PRAISE FOR
NO PERFECT PARENTS

Dave and Ann Wilson are some of our favorite people in the world, and they have been so encouraging and helpful to us in our parenting journey. Now, with this amazing book, you will understand why. They are wise, insightful, funny, and very, very real. They don't pretend to have it all together. But what they do have is a deep well of insight and experience that will make a huge difference in your parenting journey—just as they have in ours.

SHAUNTI AND JEFF FELDHAHN, social researchers and authors of *For Women Only* and *For Men Only*

When someone has traveled the road you now travel on, they just may be able to help you avoid some of the potholes. Dave and Ann Wilson don't claim to know it all, but when it comes to parenting, they do know the true source of wisdom and how to attain it. Wherever you are on the parenting journey, *No Perfect Parents* will help you leave a positive legacy.

GARY CHAPMAN, PhD, author of *The 5 Love Languages*

With their characteristic wit, wisdom, and humility, Dave and Ann Wilson reflect on decades of experience raising their own children to give parents time-tested advice and perspective. This is a fun, convicting, enjoyable, and encouraging read for all parents through all stages of parenting.

GARY THOMAS, author of *Sacred Marriage* and *Sacred Parenting*

Here's the raw, refreshing, honest look at parenting you've been hoping for. Real help from a couple who knows what you're dealing with and how to point you in the right direction as you raise your children. You will love this book.

BOB LEPINE, cohost, *FamilyLife Today*

Marriage takes work. We are so grateful we met Dave and Ann Wilson in our early years of marriage while we were still teachable. The Wilsons know marriage, and now they're helping with parenting! With seven kiddos, we are blessed to know them and have this book!

BENJAMIN AND KIRSTEN WATSON, sixteen-year NFL tight end and founders of thewatsonseven.com

NO PERFECT *Parents*

NO PERFECT *Parents*

DITCH EXPECTATIONS, EMBRACE REALITY,
AND DISCOVER THE ONE SECRET
THAT WILL CHANGE YOUR PARENTING

DAVE & ANN WILSON

WITH JOHN DRIVER

ZONDERVAN
BOOKS

ZONDERVAN BOOKS

No Perfect Parents

Requests for information should be addressed to:
Zondervan, *3900 Sparks Dr. SE, Grand Rapids, Michigan 49546*

Zondervan titles may be purchased in bulk for educational, business, fundraising, or sales promotional use. For information, please email SpecialMarkets@Zondervan.com.

ISBN 978-0-310-36224-1 (audio)

Library of Congress Cataloging-in-Publication Data

Names: Wilson, Dave, 1957 October 15- author. | Wilson, Ann, 1960- author.
Title: No perfect parents : ditch expectations, embrace reality, and discover the one secret that will change your parenting / Dave Wilson and Ann Wilson, with John Driver.
Description: Grand Rapids : Zondervan, 2021. | Includes bibliographical references. | Summary: "Raising kids with hearts for Christ is a challenge, but it's a challenge you can do. National hosts of FamilyLife Today, Dave and Ann Wilson present No Perfect Parents, a funny and engaging dialogue between their whole family with helpful applications and biblical encouragement for any parenting stage"— Provided by publisher.
Identifiers: LCCN 2020048214 (print) | LCCN 2020048215 (ebook) | ISBN 9780310362173 (hardcover) | ISBN 9780310362234 (ebook)
Subjects: LCSH: Parenting—Religious aspects—Christianity. | Child rearing—Religious aspects—Christianity.
Classification: LCC BV4529 .W579 2021 (print) | LCC BV4529 (ebook) | DDC 248.8/45—dc23
LC record available at https://lccn.loc.gov/2020048214
LC ebook record available at https://lccn.loc.gov/2020048215

Published in association with the literary agency of Wolgemuth & Associates, Inc.

Cover design: Curt Diepenhorst
Cover illustration: Ieremy | Getty Images
Interior design: Kait Lamphere

Printed in the United States of America

21 22 23 24 25 26 27 28 29 30 31 /LSC/ 15 14 13 12 11 10 9 8 7 6 5 4 3 2 1

Since this is a parenting book,
we thought it would be best
to dedicate this to our amazing parents
(all of whom are deceased except for Ann's dad)
and our growing number of grandkids.

To Dick and Toot (Ann's parents) and
Dave and Janiece (Dave's parents).
And to Olive, Porter, Holden, Bryce, Ryder, Autumn . . .
and more to come.
May you know God's love and make him known.

CONTENTS

CHAPTER 1

MONDAY NIGHT *Football and Parenting 101*

There I (Dave) was—exactly where I would spend many Sunday afternoons for the next three decades of my life: on the sidelines of the Silverdome. The stadium was nestled in Pontiac, Michigan, a suburb of Detroit about twenty miles northwest of the Motor City. After I had finished my graduate degree in theology in California, my wife, Ann, and I had just recently moved to the Detroit area, where I took a job as chaplain for the Detroit Lions—it was a dream come true.

We had only been married for six years and were beyond excited to make the move to Detroit so we could begin this new chapter in our young lives together. It was thrilling, to say the least, but I had no idea just how exhilarating it was about to become.

This wasn't a Sunday afternoon game. This was Monday Night Football. The whole world was watching in prime time as we battled one of the best teams in NFL history: the Chicago Bears. This was 1986, so the Bears were coming off a momentous season the year before that had ended with a Super Bowl trophy hoisted in their locker room. Some of you may remember the Super Bowl Shuffle—if not, look it up on YouTube and prepare to be amazed, by the fashion as much as anything else. This was the team that featured Jim McMahon, Walter Payton, and William "Refrigerator" Perry, and the head coach Mike Ditka. Needless to say, they were pretty good.

And the Lions? Well, let's just say that we were *not as good* at that point in time. In fact, someone did the math the other day and told me that after 317 losses in thirty-three seasons, I hold the dubious honor of being the losingest chaplain in NFL history . . . still waiting on my plaque to arrive in the mail. But this was early in my career, so hope still springs eternal.

The Silverdome was packed to overcapacity, with more than 85,000 screaming, face-painted, loyal Lions fans decked out from head to toe in silver and Honolulu blue (it's a real color). It was a thing of beauty. Nevertheless, we were getting killed. Shocker. But being a hopeful newbie to the organization, I put my new role as a chaplain to good use and began praying for a miracle comeback. Turns out, God was listening to my prayer and was about to use a series of unfortunate events to answer my request in an unbelievable way.

But first, things went from bad to worse—or, as Lions fans would say, the game kept going as usual. Our starting quarterback, Chuck Long, went down with an injury. His backup, Joe Ferguson, took over. In his first play under center, Joe took a shot from the legendary defensive end for the Bears, Richard Dent, who beat our right tackle and sacked him for a huge loss. Joe just lay there on the turf for a while, unable to gather himself. When he finally got back up, it was evident he wasn't going back into the game.

The thing was, for various reasons—injuries, contracts,

and whatnot—we had only two quarterbacks on the roster at the time. What were we going to do? This was a disaster. I continued to pray that something would happen to turn things around for this team.

"Wilson!"

The voice startled me. It resonated from the screaming mouth of our head coach, Darryl Rogers. I was puzzled. We had several guys with the last name Williams on our team that year, but I couldn't recall anyone named Wilson. I was looking around with the other players trying to figure out who the heck he was talking to (sorry . . . "whom" the heck).

The next thing I knew, Coach Rogers was in *my* face. "Wilson! What are you waiting for? Go suit up. You're going in at QB!"

I couldn't believe it! We were literally that desperate—and I had never been more thrilled that so many other people had suffered gruesome injuries. (Hey, I'm not proud of it.) It wasn't such a far-fetched idea that I would be an option at QB because only a few years earlier, I had finished my college career as a Hall of Fame quarterback at Ball State. My buddies now call it "Bald State" in honor of the *state* of my now nonexistent hairline. They are real good at jokes.

The point is that I had been preparing for this moment all my life, and finally, after there was literally no one left who could limp onto the field and yell "hut," a coach was forced to inadvertently reveal my incredible talent to the world.

This was really happening.

The TV time-out was extended due to the rash of injuries to our team, so I rushed to the locker room and suited up. Putting on pads again was just like riding a bike—with a different kind of helmet, of course. Before I knew it, I was fully dressed and in the huddle with the other players. My hands were shaking, but I was ready.

It was third and long and we needed a miracle to get back into this game. All Coach Rogers had said to me before sending me out onto the field as he shook his head in disbelief was, "Son, I guess . . . just, uh, let 'er rip."

I knelt down in the huddle and called for "all fades." In other words, I was going to drop back and throw a bomb to whoever was open. As I walked to the line of scrimmage, the huge crowd suddenly went silent, probably trying to figure out who number 15 was and why he was lining up under center.

I looked over at the stands to see my beautiful wife, Ann, sitting there. She looked stunned, but strangely hopeful. A single tear rolled down her perfect cheek as she mouthed the breathy words, "I love you!" I winked at her slyly, causing her to blush. Before my eyes had left hers and rotated back to the linebackers frothing at the mouth in front of me, I was already instinctively barking out the signals. A slight breeze began blowing across the field, causing the mullet hanging out of the back of my helmet to blow gently, yet majestically, in the wind.

Hut!

I took the snap and dropped back into the pocket. As expected, Dent immediately beat his guy again and was instantly barreling down on me. I had anticipated this, so I simply gave him a little juke and eluded his violent pursuit, somehow leaving him face-planted in the turf. *Still got it!* I thought to myself. But there was no time for celebration.

I had a game to win.

I looked downfield to see number 85 streaking behind the coverage. It was Jeff Chadwick. I calmly planted my front leg and launched the ball in his direction. To my surprise, it was the most beautiful post pass I had ever seen leave my hands—a perfect spiral sailing deep, deep down the left sideline. It must have traveled seventy-five yards in the air—I kid you not. It was as if the sands of time had slowed to a trickle, so much so that I could see flashing lights from the sideline photographers' cameras flickering on the immaculately rotating ball as it headed directly toward Jeff's outstretched arms.

The crowd, all 85,000 plus, began instinctively rising to their feet with a collective inhale as they anticipated what would be a historic moment. The comeback of the ages. The redemption of a franchise. The birth of a legend. The ball was mere inches from Jeff's hands as he was mere inches from the goal line. It was everything I could have ever . . .

"My water just broke!"

Wait, what?

INTERRUPTIONS AND REINTRODUCTIONS

Ann here—the mother of Dave's three children and the one who actually yelled, "My water just broke" in the middle of his obviously fantastical dream. Don't get me wrong, he was an amazing quarterback in college (with a real mullet), and I would have loved nothing more than for him to get called off the bench (basically as a spectator) into a professional football game to save the day, but guys, it didn't happen.

And yes, I do love him, but there was no single tear from the sidelines or breathy whatever-it-was he said; at that moment in our lives, we didn't have time for that.

You see, we were about to become parents.

Since then, there have been plenty of real, non-dream tears though. And laughs. And cuts and bruises. And a thousand other unexpected interruptions to our dreams and plans that we eventually realized weren't really interruptions at all; they were our real life. In fact, no series of unexpected, unpredictable, constantly interrupted experiences defines your real life—and your dreams—more than those of being a parent.

If you read our first book, *Vertical Marriage*, you know that Dave and I are often inclined to just chime in on each other's stories out of the blue, especially when *someone* is getting a little out of control with his storytelling. (Sorry, Dave . . . you know I love you, but such is life.) In terms of this book, sometimes you will hear from Dave, and sometimes you will hear from me. And sometimes you will hear from both of us at the same time.

Like right now, actually.

If, for some reason, you haven't read our first book on marriage, it may be helpful to visit at least the first few chapters to learn more about who we are and how we got here. But then again, maybe you don't have time for that right now—the kids are screaming at you from the other room as we speak. We get it, so at least let us tell you that our life together has been a wild ride full of fun, failures, and grace. We are far from perfect, and far from perfect parents, so if you share these sentiments as a parent yourself, you've come to the right place.

Writing about the topic of parenting is a daunting task, though not as daunting as the act of parenting itself. But neither is it as rewarding. Most books you read come from experts who seem to have mastered their fields of study. Sorry, but you're not going to get that from us. We only know one way to write or speak on this parenting topic—and that's with complete honesty. You will hear the highs and lows of our parenting journey, like the time one of us (who shall remain nameless for now) kicked a hole in a wall in a moment of parenting frustration. Hopefully our raw honesty will help you on your journey as well. Would you really want to hear from anyone who thinks he or she is a perfect parent? That's a perfect recipe for destruction . . . just ask our wall.

The bottom line is, we can't give you methods to guarantee you won't make mistakes as a parent or that your kids will turn out to be fun-loving, millionaire, doctoral-educated, philanthropist pastors who build homes, cure cancer, engineer the vaccine for COVID-19, and write poetry on the side. You should beware of such goals anyway (and also work on your run-on sentences). The truth is, if *you* don't make mistakes, how will *your kids* ever learn what to do when *they* make mistakes? They are watching both the good and the bad in your lives—and they need to see both, because real life has both. They don't need perfect role models; they need real ones. They need *you*, complete with all of your flaws, your personality faux pas, your inability to correctly spell *faux pas* without looking it up, and your quirkiness. *You* are the one God appointed to this job with *these* kids.

Congratulations!

You may be feeling right now what we've felt so many times over the years: that you are not enough for this task. We get it. And the truth is, you really are not enough for this undertaking—well, not by yourself anyway. No amount of study, contemplation, chart making, disciplining, rewarding, listening to podcasts, attending small groups, listening to sermons, or even reading books (including this one) is ever going to make you fully ready. The job is too big because it involves something bigger than any of us can create or manage—namely, *humans*.

Feeling confident yet? Hang on; we'll get there.

The truth is, you really *are enough* for the job, just not because you *have enough* knowledge, wisdom, or insight to do it. You absolutely do not have enough of these. But there are other reasons you are enough, which we'll get to in the coming pages. When you understand these reasons, you will be able to face the monumental task of parenting with a humble confidence to love and lead your children with an energy that is higher and longer lasting than what you get from that third cup of coffee after your kid with the flu has kept you up all night.

We believe there is a secret to parenting that most parents have never considered, and it is found in two key questions: "*What* are we trying to raise?" and "*Who* are we raising?" When those two questions are answered, we can begin to develop a plan of *how* we're going to navigate these years of parenting, regardless of *where* the varying circumstances lead.

What are we trying to raise—that is, what kind of adults do we hope our children will become? The target or bull's-eye we are shooting for is critical here, yet most parents have never really thought about this question, beyond a few standard statements we'll address.

Furthermore, it is just as important to understand who God has distinctively created your son or daughter to be. Each of your children is uniquely and beautifully designed by God with an exceptional, special identity. As parents, we can help our kids aim at the correct target by celebrating who God has made them to be while also offering them a vision for the way God wants to use them to impact the world—in big and small ways—for his good purposes.

God has something more for you as a parent—something that will help you reach past merely worrying or hoping everything will turn out okay or endlessly striving to control every detail of your children's lives. Take it from us and our mistakes—those tactics don't work. You won't—and can't—raise perfect kids, but you can embrace a perfectly healthy parenting vision of (1) knowing what your goal is in raising your kids and (2) knowing who your kids are as individuals.

Though we have other ways to say it that we'll share, this central concept remains our overall goal as parents—the target we keep trying to hit and have often missed. No, really—we know we're far from perfect parents.

In fact, just to demonstrate that we don't think we have it all together, we're inviting our three sons—CJ, Austin, and Cody—to the party. They're grown now, some with children of their own. We could wax eloquent about this and that, but let's be honest, it could very well turn out to be all just a bunch of fluff. No one has a perfect parenting story behind the closed doors of their family experience.

So we want to open the door to our home and invite you in—well, into the time-warped version of our home. We are going to invite our sons to add a few of their thoughts at the end of certain chapters and sections in this book. Some of them have a lot to say; some not so much—probably just like your kids. Regardless, who is more qualified to point out what worked and didn't work in our home than the people who were the focus of our parenting pursuits? Though their thoughts will be brief, we've not asked them to sugarcoat anything. There is no cover-up here. And at the time of this writing, we have no idea what they'll say; we've only asked them to be honest.

Honesty is what we are asking of them and of ourselves. It's what we are asking of you as well. Honesty is necessary to move from dreams flailing about in the wind of worries, hopes, and good intentions to dreams that can come true because they are grounded in a higher reality.

Speaking of dreams, back to Dave.

WAKING UP TO LEGACY

"Wake up, Dave! I said that my water just broke!" Ann was shaking me back to reality at that point. I quickly stirred to life. I remember thinking, *Water doesn't break. It pours. It spills. It flows. But it doesn't break.* And then it hit me: *we are going to have a baby . . . today!*

I was never going to know if Jeff Chadwick reeled in my perfect pass in the end zone. I did know, however, that life was about to change for the Wilsons forever. It was a frigid January morning in Michigan, but I was hot with nervous energy. We rushed to the hospital and got Ann checked into a room to get ready for the birthing process.

There were parts to getting married that were simply enchanting. The romance. The mystery. The beauty of it all. Having a baby? Not so much. It's not anyone's finest moment, to say the least. In fact, as we walked up to her room, my eyes were drawn to Ann's shoes because I kept seeing something in my peripheral vision being dragged behind her through the hospital hallway. Yeah, the item in question was her panties stuck to her heel.

Ah, an enchanted experience.

The thing about a baby being born in the modern world, especially when he or she is your first, is that it's often a process of "hurry up and wait." You spring from the bed like a madman, drive like a maniac to the hospital, rush to the room as if you're fleeing a burning building—and then you sit down and wait for fourteen or forty hours or so. Once we had Ann in her bed and hooked up to the baby monitoring machines, it became apparent that this was going to take a while.

Her nurse was confident that her labor was going to continue to be very slow. No problem. I was in this for the long haul. However, in the mad dash of getting here, I had failed to address the fact that nature was calling for me. I slipped out of the room and down the hallway to the place where many men find solace and solitude—the john. The locked bathroom even afforded me the chance to catch my breath, regain my bearings, and catch up on a little reading while I could. I left the hospital room with Ann's blessing, promising to return in just a matter of minutes.

That was my intention, but sometimes you find yourself engrossed in a really good news article and you lose track of time. Much like the scream that woke me from my football dream, a new set of screams from down the hall jarred me from my bathroom bliss . . . and these also sounded like my wife.

"Dave Wilson! Get back here *now*!"

I clumsily gathered myself and came sprinting down the hallway, entering the room just as Ann was heading into the final moments of delivery . . . thanks a lot, Nurse This-Is-Gonna-Take-a-While! Ann was none too happy with me, but soon my bathroom-based absenteeism would all fade into a distant memory. (Glad I didn't bring it back up.)

There I was. It was time. Watching (and yes, helping where I could) our first of three sons being born into the world that day was one of the most incredible moments of my life . . . even better than a perfect end zone spiral. I was now awake in more ways than one. As I held CJ in my arms, everything changed in an instant. That little five-pound, fourteen-ounce precious gift from God was my chance to leave a legacy that could impact the world in a positive way.

I had no idea they weren't going to let him stay in my arms for long because he was about to be rushed to the neonatal ICU, but from that moment forward, leaving a legacy became my new dream.

LEGACY

Legacy is one of those words that can get lost in all the feelings and impressions it produces. Much like courage, love, or hope, legacy has become the stuff of inspirational quotes and cheesy romantic comedies. But the moment I became a parent, it suddenly became very real and daunting to me. I began to explore aspects of legacy I had never thought of before—things we aim to unpack in this book.

A few decades ago (yes, I've been speaking on these topics for that long), I was talking with an elderly woman about legacy. Janiece was in her seventies and began reminiscing aloud about her life. I found out that in her late teens, she had married her husband, Ralph, who was just starting an exciting career as an airline pilot. They were young and in love, and they had the world by the tail.

It didn't take very long for them to begin having children—quite a few actually. She said they had "four jacks and a queen"—that is, four sons and a daughter. Ralph was based out of the Newark airport and also built houses on the side in the upscale parts of New Jersey. Janiece's story was an ideal picture of the life most of us want. They had the money, the big home in a gated community, the successful career, and beautiful children. It was the all-American dream.

Until it wasn't.

After nearly twenty-five years of marriage, Janiece began to suspect that her husband, now a captain with Eastern Air Lines, was having an affair when he went away on his many trips. She wasn't sure how to confirm her suspicions, so she simply made a phone call to one of the hotels where Ralph often stayed during layovers. When the hotel receptionist answered the phone, Janiece asked, "Has Captain Ralph checked in yet?"

He was a regular, so the receptionist knew who he was—and since this was long before the days of being vigilant about privacy, the receptionist unknowingly replied, "Oh, yes, he is heading to his room right now with his wife."

Janiece's heart broke into pieces inside her. When Ralph came home from that trip, she confronted him. She discovered that this affair was only one of several. Every dream she had ever known suddenly became a nightmare. As hard as they tried, they just could not save their marriage. They were divorced in 1963, and Janiece became a single mom. Her three older kids were already in college, so she moved with her two youngest sons—a seven-year-old and five-year-old—to be near her parents in another state.

Then disaster struck in ways she never imagined possible. Mere weeks after the move, she was given the news that her youngest son had leukemia. It was advanced. Within six weeks, the five-year-old was gone. As Janiece shared her story, her eyes welled up with tears. So did mine. In fact, I began to sob.

You see, Janiece is my mom, and Captain Ralph is my dad.[1]

1. My dad's full name was Ralph Dave Wilson. We all knew him as Dave, but his work associates called him Captain Ralph.

CHAPTER 2

EXPECTING THE *Unexpected*

I (Ann) held the test kit stick in my shaking hand, letting out a slow exhale. Excitement, fear, exhilaration, and panic gripped my heart as I set the stick on the counter for Dave to see.

It's okay, I reassured my thundering heart. *Just settle down in there. We got this.*

You see, I like plans. Maybe you do too. They bring such comfort, even if it's a false sense of it. They help to create expectations that can be pursued—a path that can be walked toward a destination you really want to reach. Plans are the maps by which we navigate these crazy lives . . . or at least that's the case for those of us who are planners.

For this planner, everything was going according to . . . well, you know. Dave and I would be married for five and a half years by the time the baby would be born. We were done with seminary. We would be great parents. This child would be amazing—he would be perfect, obedient, and sweet. Jesus would help us.

These were my plans, and the map looked really good on paper.

As motherhood approached, I did what any good church girl would do: I set out to find a mom's Bible study to fully prepare myself. There was safety in believing I would delve deeply into the knowledge of what was ahead. I would learn it. Apply it. Maybe even become good at it. The plans seemed to work—and my heart began to go back to its normal *bump da bump*.

I'm no cardiologist, but I'm pretty sure that's right.

A few months later, I walked into my first moms-only Bible study on parenting. The truth is, I found myself wishing that my little belly bump would protrude just a little further out so everyone would be able to more easily recognize that I was pregnant. I was a mom-to-be. I belonged here. After all, I had all these plans. The door to the meeting room was partially open, and I nudged it, holding my giant-sized Bible in my left hand, adorned in the cutest outfit I could find that morning, hoping to impress.

Chaos and what appeared to be the rubble of some WWII blitzkrieg lay before me. Toys, bottles, blankets, burp rags, laughing children, screaming babies, car seats, infant swings, high chairs, and moms talking very loudly so they could hear one another above the sirens of the children's cries met my shocked gaze. *What the heck had I gotten myself into? Was this going to be my life?*

No! Surely, it won't be like this for me, I thought to myself as the aroma of the spit-up cascading down the young woman's shoulder next to me wafted in my direction. She seemed to not even notice it, even though it was nothing less than something you might smell from a putrid, rancid dumpster sitting in the hot sun filled with open bottles of expired milk. Surely this was not the smell of motherhood—the one to which we all eventually go "noseblind." Poor soul—there was an actual Cheerio clinging to a tendril of her ponytail that was flopping halfway out of its band. She just kept her eyes forward, ignoring the mayhem around her—and yes, the mayhem literally *on* her.

Come on girls, I thought. *Have some pride!*

And what were they wearing? One girl looked as if she had pulled her shirt from the bottom of the laundry basket that morning—a laundry basket that had been full for many, many mornings. It also looked like it may have been her husband's shirt. Again, she didn't seem to even notice. Well, I *would never* let myself fall into this kind of motherly disrepair. I was aghast. I was appalled. I was arrogant.

I was also wrong.

As I recall my naivety in those days, I can't help but laugh. I had so many expectations of what parenting would look like and what kind of children I would raise. I had expectations of what I would be like as a mom. I seriously thought I would be able to control everything that was to come. I had conquered other giants—this one would go down just as easily. I would prevail, and it would be fine.

And I was fine, so to speak. But I had to painfully redefine my expectations for the term *fine* as it relates to parenting. Within a few short months and in the years that followed my first exposure to that veritable field hospital of motherhood, I became every mom in that room. But oddly enough, I felt no shame in it. I didn't always like the smell, but there are a lot worse things in life than going noseblind.

I learned to embrace the blindness.

Even so, there is some blindness you shouldn't embrace—namely, the blindness of expectations. Expectations can keep you from seeing clearly the life ahead of you because you can only see the life that exists in your imagination. Dave and I have both met moms and dads who seem to be walking into parenthood carrying (and even protecting) a specific image of what their children will be like and how they will turn out. Not only that, they guard a mental image of what the mother or father of their children will be like when the roles are finally in place.

You may be new to the game of parenting, or you may be an old pro. Regardless, before we attempt to delve into any specifics of what to do as a parent, may I offer some insight from a friend who has struggled with plans and expectations at every stage of this parenting thing? It would be best to just ditch your expectations *now.*

If you don't empty yourself of rigid expectations and set new expectations that are based on principles and boundaries, not rules and guarantees, then you will only be disillusioned and disappointed in yourself and your kids—and all for no reason. Real life was always going to happen; you just didn't expect it for what it was—namely, *unpredictable.*

WHAT EVERY PARENT HATES TO DO: SURRENDER

One evening, Dave and I happened to get messages from all of our then-adult children, and each of them sent a picture of what they were doing. CJ and Robin, who don't have children, were watching an epic movie on their large-screen HDTV. Cody and Jenna, who at that point had one son who was so young that he was still sleeping more than twelve hours a day and couldn't even roll over, much less run around the house, were spending one of his naptimes reading their Bibles in their peaceful and tidy house while a worship band could be seen playing on the TV screen in the background.

Then came Austin and Kendall's picture. You see, they have

littles . . . active littles. We had to zoom in to see if what we thought we were seeing was actually there. Was that actually a Little Tikes slide teetering on their bed? Was that actually three-year-old Olive reaching down to help her year-and-a-half-old brother, Porter, scale Pillow Mountain to reach the turnstiles at the top, the best ride in their own little self-made amusement park?

In both cases, the answer was yes. Pillows of all sizes had been gathered from the four corners of the earth and piled on the floor below the slide to ensure a safe and luxurious landing for every little adventurous rider. Kendall was smiling, standing to the side and holding their new, sleeping foster baby in her arms. Austin was the animated amusement park director and host, gleefully helping his two young guests experience the most dangerous (yet safest) ride of their *whole lives* (to date, which wasn't very long . . . just don't tell them that).

Whether you're an expectant parent, a brand-new parent, a parent of multiple littles, or a parent with teens or young adults who is holding on for dear life, you are never stagnant in your journey as a parent. You are always moving from one stage to another. You are always exiting something and entering something else. And if you're like us, you often don't know what you're doing!

No one prepared me—and perhaps nothing *can* prepare you—for the onslaught of emotions, the endless days, the sleepless nights, the joy of victory, and the agony of defeat that comes with parenting. I wish I could tell you that as they get older, you will stop worrying as much, stop painfully loving as much, or stop fighting the temptation to control something (even if only a small something) in your kids' lives. This simply is not the case. This amusement park has no closing time—it is a lifelong adventure.

So from the outset of our journey through these pages, let us invite you to take a step toward health—to do one thing we are often still learning the hard way: choose to *surrender*. We know this word can have religious undertones that may either deeply resonate with you or deeply repel you. We invite you to reject either option. Just take in the word with its simplest meaning: to throw up your hands and offer full control to another.

This has been more difficult for me because I tend to be more controlling than Dave. I could say this is more common for moms, and this may be true statistically, but I don't think it's about men and women. Each of us has a unique wiring, and some of us really want to forecast the dangers ahead, mitigate them by planning alternate routes, and ultimately keep some semblance of control.

Control is what we really want, but it's the one thing we actually do not have, no matter how much we imagine or strive to do. From day one, children reveal this very truth (that we are out of control) more than almost any other experience in our lives. *Surrender* is just one simple word, but it is by far the most difficult action step you will take as a parent—and you will need to take it over and over again.

We'd like to help you take that step so that before we ever discuss any practical parenting concepts, you'll have the right expectations of how and where to apply them in a life you've already acknowledged is not under your control at all.

SURRENDERING EXPECTATIONS

If you're like me, maybe you're saying, "Wait, what? How can I surrender when I'm in charge? I run the house, and I set the rules. *Surrender* is a nice-sounding metaphorical concept, but someone's got to get the kids registered for preschool, clean the house, referee the constant fighting, reconcile the incorrect EOBs from the pediatrician, and the like. No time for high-falutin niceties. Call me when you have some concrete tips for keeping my sanity."

All valid points, my friend. I get it. Even so, and this may be difficult to accept, true surrender is the only path that leads to maintaining your sanity. However, it's also the only way to accomplish a lifelong mission that is greater than simply keeping your kids alive, fed, and enrolled in school and sports. It begins with seeking to understand the boundaries that exist between *your* role and *God's* role. And yes, such a concrete thing does exist. The other side of Dave's opening story about CJ's birth might help.

The trip to the hospital that cold night was truly unexpected because CJ was coming three weeks early. After registering at the front desk, the nurse checked me into my room with a bored and tired look. I understood. It was about three in the morning, and she had probably helped hundreds of babies come into the world just that week. I sheepishly asked her if she thought I would deliver anytime soon, having no idea what to expect and thinking I could help control the situation if I knew the plan ahead. I was already a little off-kilter since my due date wasn't for three more weeks. Going into labor this early was not the plan.

"Oh, honey, don't get your hopes up," she said. "By the look of things, I'd say it's gonna be another twenty-four hours before that baby takes his first breath."

Ugh, that was not what I wanted to hear. I was disappointed, to say the least, but I tried to readjust my expectations. Dave, on the other hand, grabbed a magazine and headed to the bathroom. After all, he had all the time in the world.

After they hooked me up to a fetal monitor, I was able to hear CJ's precious little heartbeat. The hospital was very quiet, and I was in the room alone, so it was soothing music to my ears. Soon I would hold him in my arms. Then suddenly, it felt like my contractions were coming at closer and closer intervals. They were also *much* more painful. The nurse had told me she would call the doctor when the contractions were getting closer, probably sometime into the evening to come.

I tried to relax, but this was seriously hurting! Was I supposed to endure this for another twenty-four hours? I leaned forward as the next contraction came, invoking my newly learned breathing methods. *How long has Dave been gone? Woooooo, here comes another contraction! Wow!* This wasn't how I pictured having a baby! I imagined Dave by my side cheering me on as the nurse said, "Wow, you're doing great, honey!"

But instead, it was just me and that stupid strap around my belly. The next contraction caused me to break into a sweat, soaking my forehead. But what grabbed my full attention was the fact that I could barely hear our baby's heartbeat through the monitor during these moments of intense pain.

Is that normal? I wondered, gulping a big breath of air as the contraction subsided. I looked at the stream of paper flowing out of the fetal monitor and could see that the heart rate had become weaker and that there was a long space between beats during each contraction.

Where was everyone anyway?

I finally pushed the button for the nurse, embarrassed that I needed her after only fifteen minutes in the room. I reassured myself that I was just a rookie. It was okay to ask if this was normal and if everything was okay with the baby. Another contraction hit just as the nurse nonchalantly walked into the room. She pulled a rubber glove onto her hand and gave me a smug look as if I was exaggerating the pain.

The contraction subsided as she approached the bedside. I looked up at her and apologized for hitting my button. "I know you said I wouldn't have this baby for another twenty-four hours, but I have two questions. One, is it normal for a baby's heart rate to become so weak during a contraction? And two, is it normal that it seems like I have to push alreeeeeeaaadddyy?" Another contraction hit me as I was talking. I was bearing down and gripped by pain. How did women actually live through this?

She rolled her eyes again as she moved over to the monitor tape. I watched her gaze as she heard and now saw CJ's heart rate dip down and soften. Suddenly there was alarm in her eyes. She now looked intently at me as I was pushing. She hustled to the end of the bed and checked me.

"The baby is coming out. Don't push!" she screamed as she ran out the door. "I need to call the doctor!"

My mind began to panic. *She hadn't called the doctor yet? Was something wrong? Why is the baby's heart rate dipping? Where is my husband?*

"Dave Wilson, get in here now!" I screamed.

As you already know, Dave sprinted down the hall and made it in time to be with me for CJ's birth. The doctor caught the tail end of the experience. As it turned out, CJ's umbilical cord was wrapped around his neck, which was causing his heart rate to dip. Because of this, as soon as he was born, they rushed him to the NICU without either of us being able to see him, much less hold him.

This was *not* the way I had expected parenthood to begin.

As we waited on pins and needles for the doctor to arrive with news about our little CJ, we held hands in silence. We had prayed over this baby every single day, multiple times a day. I never knew I could love and care for someone so much before even meeting them. In fact, as you read this, maybe your story has tragic similarities. As we write about parenting, maybe your parent heart is wounded in a way that feels beyond repair. Our hearts deeply hurt with you—and with every parent who has lost a child before or after birth. The love we experience as parents is a force to be reckoned with, whether the baby is still in the womb or has breathed their first breath.

Austin and Kendall had three miscarriages before Olive was born. Those three precious lives were their first three children—and our first three grandchildren. It was agonizing for them, and for us. At times it still is.

The bottom line is that just the potential to become a parent carries with it both the potential for the greatest joy in life, as well as for the deepest heartache. You can't have one without the other.

Only mere minutes after CJ's birth, we were definitely feeling the *other*.

After what seemed like an eternity, a doctor we had never met finally walked through the door and introduced himself. My eyes were searching his face for any clue to our son's condition.

"Congratulations, your son is doing well," he said. I finally exhaled a breath I had been unknowingly holding for God knows how long, squeezing Dave's hand in relief. He continued. "We just want to run a few more tests to make sure he doesn't have a skull fracture due to the very fast labor and delivery." With that, he walked out of the room.

A skull fracture?

I quickly turned to Dave, "Have you ever heard of a baby having a skull fracture?"

"No!" His look was grim. "I'm going to try to find out more about what's going on." He walked out behind the doctor.

I was suddenly left alone in the stillness of the hospital room.

"God, are you here?" I quietly whispered. "Do you see what's going on?" Tears welled up and began to involuntarily overflow onto my hospital gown. I was frantic with a worry I had never experienced. A fierce protection was already welling up within me. I knew Dave felt it too as he marched out of the room. I would die for this child right now to protect his life, yet I felt helpless and unable to do anything for him but pray.

Surrender him to me, Ann.

I'm not saying I heard the voice of God audibly, but in that moment of complete crisis, I knew as clear as day that God was whispering directly to my spirit. I've heard him say those words before—in my marriage and in many other parts of my own life. In fact, if you know anything about our story, you know that Dave and I both heard a similar whisper on our tenth anniversary when, unbeknownst to Dave, our marriage was on the verge of collapse. This was when we realized that all of our "horizontal" efforts in our marriage, relationships, work pursuits, church, and the like had limits—we couldn't produce in our lives or ourselves what we most deeply desired to be or to do. As the apostle Paul wrote, "I have the desire to do what is right, but not the ability to carry it out" (Romans 7:18 ESV).

We have good desires, but we do not have the ability to do them—to grow healthy marriages, to overcome our addictions, to heal from our childhood wounds, and, most certainly, to raise our children to become the people they have the potential to become. We see it. We want it. And yet we can't do it.

For our marriage, we heard the whisper and surrendered to it—that is, we went *vertical*, trusting God to do in us what we had finally realized we could never do in ourselves. *Vertical* is a term we use to describe the pursuit of finding life, happiness, and real power to keep growing, putting a vertical relationship with Jesus ahead of all other relationships. Yet even when we surrendered to the vertical, it didn't make things perfect. It certainly didn't remove the pain or the struggle. Instead, it gave purpose to the pain and struggle because we had better tools of grace and trust to invite God into those moments. Instead of hiding in our darkness, we brought God into the darkness—and he began to bring his light, healing, and power to our shadows.

Again, I had prayed prayers like these before and would pray many more in the future (the tenth anniversary was years after this moment), but this surrendering of my helpless little baby was different. This child would need me, literally depending on me to live. How could I surrender him? I felt so helpless, lost, and desperate. Could I really surrender this newborn into God's hands, not knowing the outcome—not knowing if God would do with his life all that I most hoped he would do?

It was a scary thought, and I wrestled with it—just as I continue to wrestle with it every day. Even so, after only twenty-five brief years of life, I had at least come to recognize and believe that God loved me, loved Dave, and loved this child we had prayed for. I also believed that in the end, God's plan for my child was better than mine, no matter how hard that plan might be to accept—something much easier said than done . . . right, Mom? It was hard, but I knew God was the only perfect parent in our situation.

"God, I am petrified," I prayed. "But I give you our baby, and I'm begging you to let him be okay. Even so, I trust you, no matter the outcome, and I place him and his future into your loving arms." In my mind, I was placing CJ on a sacred altar, pleading with God to let him live and be healthy.

I would pray the same prayer at Austin's birth, who was born six and a half weeks early and spent time in the NICU. I prayed it over Cody when I went into labor with him at only twenty-one weeks. I was put on complete bed rest until he was born at thirty-seven weeks. He was also placed in the NICU when he stopped breathing after birth.

You see, these are only a few of the countless moments of surrender we've faced during our parenting years. I'm guessing you have your own scary moments as well. Our years have been filled with earnest, often fearful prayers of continually surrendering our children and their lives to Jesus. It was—and remains—the hardest act I've ever done in my life.

This is hard for all of us, no matter our situation. In fact, we should take this moment early in these pages to acknowledge a few key things about our varying circumstances. Parents do not all have the same situations. We are going to write from the perspective of having remained married (this almost didn't happen) for most of our lives. We realize you may be a single parent, a divorced person, a parent navigating a blended situation within multiple families, a widow or widower, an adoptive or foster parent, or even a grandparent or other family member raising a child you never expected to have in your home.

Hear our hearts. No matter your situation, your value as a parent is equal to anyone else's and is important to God. You don't have to fit into our family's box (a long-term marriage) or into anyone else's box to be able to apply the principles we will be discussing. This will mean you will have to extract and adapt various truths and principles from our stories so you can apply them to your own.

When we are overwhelmed or feel unseen or unheard, we want to cry out, "My situation is too different! I'm alone." Or divorced, widowed, single, adopting, mourning the loss of one of your children, lovingly raising a special needs child, or a hundred other scenarios. Instead of feeling so alone due to your circumstances, we invite you to listen to the mistakes and perspectives from our stories and apply from them what works for you. Just like parenting, this will be an integrative process. You will have to adapt on the fly.

We are parents to three sons. We had no real choice in this, but it may be tempting to think that our experiences can't be applied to your life if you are the parent of daughters. We want you to know we see and hear you as well. I (Ann) know what it's like to be a daughter and a mother. Also, as pastors living in community for more than thirty years, we have walked with many families and many young women through their various issues and seasons of life. No one is a specialist in parenting, but we also don't want you to think we have no experience here. We are *so* willing to share our mistakes, as they are the most effective experiences you can learn from and hopefully avoid. Regardless, I hope that my (Ann's) voice and experiences, and our intentional adaptation of certain concepts to equally apply to females, will be enjoyable and helpful to parents who have boys, girls, or both.

Depending on your own life, you may also be tempted to feel emotionally disconnected from our story because your own relationship status as an adult is different or broken. While it is true that no one can write something that spans everyone's unique background and experiences, we want you to know that our story is not as squeaky-clean as it may appear at first glance.

I (Dave) come from a broken home where adultery and addiction defined much of my childhood. I was raised by a single mom, and I lost a brother to cancer. I have struggled with pride, pornography, emotional detachment, and a lot more you'll learn about in the pages to come.

And I (Ann) come from a home of loving parents who stayed together and made my childhood such a fun and accepting place. Still, my parents didn't really hug or kiss me past the fourth grade. In our family, you were expected to win at everything you tried, so I became insecure, driven, and controlling, and I eventually sought love and affection through promiscuity, which only left me more broken. I also experienced sexual abuse.

Yeah, the Wilsons have carried their own share of baggage —and while we won't unpack all of it in this book (there's just not enough time for everything), we want you to know that brokenness is universal, so you don't have to feel alone in yours, even if your story differs from ours. You also don't have to repeat the story you came from—God wants to help you change your family's legacy.

Finally, you may be reading this as a parent of a prodigal. Every page, with its honest and sometimes funny stories, may feel like a dagger to your soul. Again, our sons are far from perfect and each have their own issues. Even so, we acknowledge that your situation may feel more immediately dreadful than ours. We don't have all the answers, and we promise not to whitewash our parenting stories, reminding you of everything we did right and everything you did wrong to get to where you are.

There are no perfect parents, but there is hope, even for those who are far from the right path. We hurt with you and invite you to sit at this table with the rest of us. You belong— and we're all learning to keep surrendering our broken lives and situations. It's not too late, and much of this book will deal with parents as they listen, learn, and make changes (after all, most of our kids will never read it). Maybe something here will offer you a prayerful first step to seeing God bring incredible healing into your broken situation. Let us invite you to join us and to keep on hoping.

This won't be a book focused on lists, gotchas, and implementable steps, though there will be some of these. Rather, we want to help you find hope and strength from the One who loves your kids more than you do—to point you toward his principles and plan to guide your parenting. When you discover God's bull's-eye for your children (mission) and combine it with who God created them to be (identity), you will have a road map for your parenting journey. It doesn't necessarily make the task easier, but it does give you hope and a path to cling to in the middle of endless chaos.

You can build a great house that may *stand* for a long time, but unless it is built on a solid foundation, it won't be able to *withstand* those moments when storms beat against it. And trust us, being a parent means a lot of storms are coming, from hospitals to hormones to promposals to potential pain and joy and life beyond your wildest imagination.

Breathe. It will all come in its own time. Whether our children are newborns or already have children of their own, *this moment* is the only place we can begin. We invite you to pray with us the simple prayer in your own words that we have prayed every day since we began our journey as parents. Fight the desire to be the sole protector for your children—you know you are not enough to do this. You can't control circumstances, keep them from pain, or create teachable, contrite, engaged hearts within them. Our horizontal actions matter, but our vertical foundation matters so much more.

Let it begin (or begin again) today with a simple surrender. If you're not sure how to do this, these words may give you a few ideas:

God, I recognize that I am not able to do this job of parenting in a way that ensures a positive result. It takes too much worry, fear, and control to even try. I don't know how to do it, but I choose to surrender to you. I ask you to be in charge of my life, my marriage, my situation, my kids, and my heart. Amen.

CHAPTER 3

THE PARENTING SECRET *That Changes Everything*

As Ann described, we had more than one close call in the hospital with the birth of our three sons, CJ, Austin, and Cody. We know that many hearts have been broken over stories like these that don't turn out the way we all want them to. We hurt with you. In our story, we don't know why things turned out the way they did, so we remain humbly grateful every day that God spared our three sons and let each of them grow up to become healthy men with families of their own.

I (Dave) personally know the pain of the alternative very well. Again, I was the seven-year-old who moved with my mother after the traumatic divorce that devastated our family. Craig was my little brother—and my best friend. I thought things couldn't get worse after the separation of my parents. I was wrong. When Craig became sick, it felt like there was no time to process. He died just weeks after our move. Everything in my life had changed in ways I couldn't even begin to process as a seven-year-old little boy.

Our first son, CJ, is named after my brother Craig—a tribute to his short life. I can still feel the pain of losing him as I write these words. I also share the experiences of what it's like to be raised by a single parent. It was hard on my mom in ways I couldn't fully see until I was a parent myself. So if you're doing this parenting thing all by yourself, you are my hero. We pray that the stories and insights in the pages to come will help you know that you don't have to lose hope—no matter how hard it is, you don't have to give up. I promise you that there were many times when my mom *thought* I would never amount to anything good, but let me add that she never once shared *with me* any disappointment she might have been feeling *in me*. Did you catch that? There was not one single time when she *said* I would not amount to anything great. She continually believed in me and spoke words of life to me—so often that, over time, I began to believe them myself. God used her love and perseverance to help mold me into the man I am today.

He will use you too.

My family was devastated by the breakup, but divorce wasn't our only dagger. There was a lot of baggage in my family's genes. Our story and issues of origin were deep wells that contained painful patterns of addiction and abandonment. I'm guessing the same may be true for your family. My mother and father both struggled with alcohol abuse. Adultery abounded for years. Fights and loud screaming were practically everyday occurrences. These were not patterns they developed for themselves; they were just following in the footsteps of their own families. We all tend to pick up our family's legacy, unless we intentionally allow our vertical relationship with God to intersect and alter our horizontal stories and patterns.

We must see our legacies for what they are before we can even dream of seeing them change for the better.

After the divorce, my dad didn't visit often. When he did, like clockwork, he would drink too much and become increasingly angry. Things usually escalated quickly and got ugly—fast. I would run to my little bedroom in the back corner of the house and cover my ears until it was over. It usually lasted for several hours. These are my most lasting and impressionable memories of my dad.

I resented him so much for all the pain he caused us. I was angry with him, and rightly so. I just didn't realize that the anger I felt *toward him* was the same anger I had inherited *from him*. We like to think it's different, and it may very well exist for different reasons, but anger—or lust, abuse, pride, selfishness, addiction, and the like—is still in the same family where the anger originated. No matter what its expression may look like, when you fight fire with fire, you just catch more things on fire.

I was on fire, just as my father was; I just didn't realize it. After I graduated from high school and left home for college on a football scholarship, I really began to copy the sins of my father. At that point in my life, I had never really read the Bible and didn't even know that God says, "I lay the sins of the parents upon their children; the entire family is affected—even children in the third and fourth generations" (Exodus 20:5 NLT).

This is a difficult verse, but in context today, it doesn't mean I was cursed or destined to make bad choices beyond my control. The choices were all mine, as were the consequences for them. Rather, this verse reminds me that there are patterns of evil chasing after me—molds into which I was poured as a child that threatened to harden me into the same shape of those whose anger and addiction had defined my childhood experiences. I was inheriting something from my parents in ways I didn't yet realize.

And I also didn't yet realize I could break that mold.

As I moved into my junior year at Ball State University, I had become a womanizing, beer-drinking party animal who believed that girls, football success, and money could bring me happiness. (*I wonder where I learned all that from.*) Unless something changed, I was destined—because I had given in to my family's patterns and ultimately agreed to destine myself—to become the spitting image of my father, a man I had vowed to never become. I was on a fast track to the same life, and I didn't even know it. And at the time, I would have denied it was happening.

I was bound to the legacy of my father. Maybe you know the feeling.

But what if I told you that you don't have to be confined to the legacy of your family? Better yet, what if I told you that you are also not bound to repeat the passing down of that legacy to your own children?

Fast-forward to January 1986 and a hospital room in Michigan. I found myself holding my first son, and it hit me. He is my chance to rewrite the legacy of the Wilson name. Our name had been associated with alcohol, adultery, and womanizing, but now Ann and I had been given the opportunity to write a new future. I didn't have the right pen or ink to do so, but God did. Though I didn't know it in that moment, changing my family's legacy would be at the center of his call on my life.

Ann and I will be the first to tell you we have not created a perfect legacy. Our three sons and five grandkids are not flawless. They are amazing people, but far from perfect—and they would be the first to agree. Yet as we watch our sons and their families live their lives, there is a new foundation on which the Wilson name is being built, even when what is being built is less than perfect.

Maybe your life looks like the all-American dream. Maybe

you're expecting your first child, filling a perfect nursery with the perfect baby furniture. Or maybe you're overrun by wild, sweet, screaming, crying, loving, hurting, sick, fun, anxious, sometimes surprisingly mean, sometimes surprisingly insightful kids on all sides—and you're not really sure what you're even aiming for as a parent, besides survival . . . and I mean for you as much as for your children. Maybe you're a single parent, a divorced parent, a blended parent, or a married parent—just trying to find your way.

We don't have all the answers, but we'd be honored to explore the questions with you (and struggle and hope and laugh alongside you) as we all seek to create the right legacy—one that honors Christ and makes a lasting, positive impact on the world. A legacy that may seem impossible to even imagine in your present state.

I get it. I was a lost cause.

BUT GOD

A passage in the book of Ephesians describes my life during those college years to a tee. The apostle Paul writes, "As for you, you were dead in your transgressions and sins, in which you used to live when you followed the ways of this world . . . gratifying the cravings of our flesh and following its desires and thoughts" (Ephesians 2:1–3). If something radical didn't happen, I was going to end up becoming a clone of my dad.

But the next two words Paul writes changes everything: "But God . . ." Paul says, "*But God*, being rich in mercy, because of the great love with which he loved us, even when we were dead in our trespasses, made us alive together with Christ—by grace you have been saved" (Ephesians 2:4–5 ESV, emphasis mine). "But God" is the ultimate combination of words that reverses expectations and brings hope to any situation that seems beyond repair.

Going into my junior football season, I was a preseason All-American pick, which meant I was considered one of the best quarterbacks in the nation. Everything was as perfect as it could be. I had success on the field, a bit of fame, women, parties—and I even still had a bit of hair. (Actually it was only a single bang, but I combed it over as far as it would go!) Despite everything that seemed to be going right, by the end of that season, I had ended up in the hospital for my second knee surgery. I had also lost my starting quarterback job. To top it all off, I walked in on my girlfriend—the woman I was planning to marry—with another guy.

I was crushed and didn't know where to turn.

At that point in my life, I thought Jesus and religion were for losers who were weak and needed help. I was a winner who had my life together, and I wasn't about to become one of those nerdy Christians I saw around campus. They were a bunch of rule followers who had no fun and no life.

What an arrogant punk I was!

Today I am so grateful that God loved me in the middle of my rebellion and pride. I remember lying in my hospital bed at Ball Memorial Hospital in Muncie, Indiana, and yelling at God for screwing up my life. "Why did you let my little brother die? Why did you let my dad leave? Why am I here in this hospital again for another knee surgery? Why am I so unhappy?"

Ann talked about surrender. Well, there was no way I was surrendering my life to the very God who was responsible for causing so much pain in my life. I may have thought I was far away from surrender, but desperation has a way of bringing us closer to truth and health than we sometimes realize. I also think that not having the ability to play football took away a lot of the sideways energy that had kept me in perpetual motion. Being laid up forced me to stop and be alone with my thoughts.

As I got out of the hospital and started to rehab my knee, I also began the work needed to rehab my life. There are too many details to recount, but after many long conversations and times of honest self-reflection, I discovered that most of the things I was investing my life in were not giving me life in return; they were giving me death instead. Just like Dad. My attitude. My relationships. My mental health. All that "living it up" was killing me, just as Ephesians 2:3 had described.

Then my "but God" moment happened. I finally realized that another touchdown pass, another girl, or another beer was never going to satisfy the longings of my heart. If I didn't discover what would give me true life, I was going to end up just like my father.

My older brother, Rob, had become a Christ follower and shared the gospel with me. I remember one of the verses that stuck out from our conversations: "I have come that they may have life, and have it to the full" (John 10:10). This communicated that God actually wanted me to have a full life, not an empty one, which challenged my view of him. At that time in my life, I believed that Christians had no freedom (just a bunch of rules to follow), no fun (I had never seen a Christian really laugh), and no fulfillment (I couldn't name a single Christian man I respected). Who would sign up for that kind of life?

But I discovered I couldn't have been more wrong about the Christian life. I realized I had been searching for life and happiness in all the wrong places. The God I was so mad at was actually the God who wanted to bring me the happiness (what I was defining as freedom, fun, and fulfillment) I was so desperately seeking. As I surrendered my life and future to

Jesus, I had no idea how that decision would alter not only my life but the lives of my future children as well.

When CJ was born more than thirty-four years ago, we decided we weren't going to try to raise our family under our own strength. After all, we learned in the delivery room that we were not in control. We needed help—and I had become confident that God really wanted to offer this help. Ann and I chose (and continue to choose) to surrender our marriage to Jesus, which is our definition of what it means to go vertical. We also chose to surrender our kids to Jesus. We can't raise children or grandchildren without his help, so we pray together every day and invite Jesus to do what only he can do.

It hasn't been easy, but God has answered our prayer. We've failed many times, but since he's in charge, our failures don't have to define our family. His love for us is our foundation. For the last thirty-four years, I have chosen to fast on Fridays for my boys—and now their wives and my grandkids as well. I abstain from food all day, and every time I have a hunger pang, which is quite often, I pray for each of my kids. These times of prayer are like a journal in my head. I remember praying for each of my sons' wives before these women were ever born. Ann and I still pray together every day for our kids, and the weekly fast day has become a ritual I still look forward to.

Each of my sons' wedding days was an emotional moment for me. Not only was I the father of the groom, but I also had the honor of being the officiating pastor. As I looked into the eyes of Kendall and then Robin and then Jenna, I knew I was looking at a precious woman of God who is an answer to our many prayers. As you'll see in the following pages, Ann and I are broken people with all kinds of flaws and weaknesses. Rather than hiding these flaws, we keep bringing them to an awesome, almighty, loving Father who is our ever-present and willing help in times of trouble (Psalm 46). He can do beyond what we can only dream or wish for (Ephesians 3:20).

Since I now have grown kids and grandkids, I stand at a season that is on the back end of the whole parenting thing—and I want to share all of these experiences behind me and around me to encourage you as someone who may be in the early stages or in a stage of crisis. We still have crises, but we now have more answered prayers behind us than before us—and that is a testament to the faithfulness of our God and his love for us and our children. No matter what you're facing, we genuinely pray that you will go vertical and surrender your life and legacy to the only One who can truly make a difference.

Once you do, you're ready to begin taking aim at all the things this surrender can produce.

SHARPEN YOUR AIM

Several years ago, Ann and I were kicking off a series called Vertical Family at our church, Kensington Church, at our Saturday night service. I was a bit more nervous than usual that night because this message was being taped live, which meant there would be no edits made before it would be shown the next morning to our other seven campus locations. We only had one shot to get it right, and I didn't want to mess it up. Every word required tact, nuance, and precision.

As we began, Ann asked me what I remembered most about raising our kids when they were young. In my brilliant mind, I wanted to say, "When our kids were toddlers, I remember thinking I'd never take another *nap* for the rest of my life." Parents of young children know exactly what I'm talking about. It's exhausting, and we never seem to get a moment to ourselves. It was going to be a valid point that resonated with the listeners.

However, what actually came out of my mouth onstage was, "When our kids were toddlers, I remember thinking I'd never take another *crap* for the rest of my life." Oh what a difference a few consonants make! The audience roared with laughter. Ann almost fell off her stool. I sheepishly asked the video team if they could edit the line before showing the video to almost fifteen thousand church attenders the next day. No such luck. They kept it in the video message for days to follow, so I received numerous texts that asked, "Have you taken a crap yet?"

And in case you are wondering, the answer is yes. Many since then, in fact . . . and now this gross subject has been brought into a respectable book. I hope you're happy.

Regardless of what I said, what I meant to say is so very true. Parenting can be exhausting at times, especially when our kids are young. It often feels like the days will never end. But now as an empty nester, I walk around an empty house and often find myself longing for those days.

When we were young parents, older parents often warned us to enjoy our moments with our little kids because we would blink and they'd be gone. We would sigh when our boys threw something sharp at one another or wiped more snot on our legs, dreaming about having a quiet house one day—and yes, using the bathroom uninterrupted. But guess what? The older parents were right! We blinked, and now they are gone. It seems like yesterday that our house was full of chaos, with toys and balls and furry animals scattered everywhere that needed to be picked up each night (if we could find them, that is). But now we are the "older" couple, and we're telling you what was told to us because it's true: your time with your kids is limited.

Since this is true, let us also share ways to maximize the time you have while you still have it. When Ann and I do parenting conferences, we always start with a crucial series of questions that few parents ever seem to ask: "In raising your children, what are you shooting for? What's your target . . . your bull's-eye?"

We must have a target to aim at, or we will just fire aimlessly. One Friday when our three boys were very young, Ann and I picked them up after school and drove to their grandparents' house for the weekend. I was driving the minivan and became super sleepy, so I asked Ann if she'd be willing to drive so I could take a nap (notice I said *nap*). Ann immediately and excitedly said yes, because every parent knows when you're traveling with young kids, the best seat in the vehicle is the driver's seat. The parent in the passenger seat has to deal with whatever has to be taken care of with the kids; the driver just has to keep it between the lines.

All three boys were asleep at this moment, so I knew it was a good time for me to get a little shut-eye myself. We pulled over to the shoulder of the road and switched seats. As soon as I had tilted my seat back, three-year-old Austin said, "I have to go potty!"

Now, many parents out there would pull into a rest stop and find a bathroom for their child, but not the Wilsons! We had all boys, and I was always in a race to beat my most recent time to get to each and every destination, so we *never* stopped for potty breaks. Instead, we carried a large coffee can that the boys could use while we kept driving. I know it sounds a little (or a lot) barbaric, but it worked, and we always made record time, which was really important to Ann. (Yeah, certainly Ann.)

Ann nudged me to take care of Austin, but I was almost half asleep so I wasn't responding very quickly. By the time I reached around and took the lid off the can, Austin had pulled down his pants and was ready to go—and I mean *really* ready. Before I could get the can into position, he was already firing away and missed the can completely.

His target? Yep, you guessed it. He hit me right between the eyes. And because of the awkward layout of our whole shenanigans, it was a good two seconds before I could divert the stream away from my head and into the can. To this day, I believe this was the moment I began to lose my hair. Ann laughed so hard that she almost ran the car off the road.

I learned two lessons that day. The first one was to never relinquish the driver's seat, no matter how tired you may be. There are worse things than being tired.

The other? Targets *really* matter.

When it comes to raising our kids, it's very important to know what we are aiming for. This may sound elementary and unnecessary, but take it from someone who has asked thousands of parents the question of what they're aiming for. Most parents we've met have never even considered it. Instead, they just live according to some hopeful, wishful thinking that their kids will somehow randomly turn out well.

When we ask parents what they hope for, we hear words like these:

- *successful* (whatever that means)
- *happy* (who defines what that is?)
- *well-adjusted* (adjusted to what?)
- *popular* (do we really want that?)

I think as parents, we can often set the bar too low—and far too nonspecific. God has a dream for your children that is a much better bull's-eye to shoot for. The principle for finding the right target comes from Scripture:

> Unless the LORD builds the house,
> the builders labor in vain . . .
> Children are a heritage from the LORD,
> offspring a reward from him.
> *Like arrows in the hands of a warrior*
> *are children born in one's youth.*
> Blessed is the man
> whose quiver is full of them.
>
> *Psalm 127:1, 3–5, emphasis mine*

God's perspective is that our children are a blessing from him and that they are like arrows, which means they are made to move somewhere specific and do something useful with their lives. So the question is this: What is a good bull's-eye to aim at when raising our children?

When our boys were super young, Ann and I wrote out a mission statement as a target to shoot at. You may not be into mission statements (neither are we), but hear us out. A specific statement helped us know what to begin doing—and how to keep adjusting our strategy as things changed. This way, we wouldn't just be reacting to what was happening to our kids. We were also attempting to help make something happen with them.

A strategy for parenting is a lot like the mission plan in the middle of *Saving Private Ryan*. The circumstances and terrain are going to change in ways you can't predict, but when you know what direction to keep heading in, even when you have to temporarily divert at times, you'll be able to stay on course toward an actual goal. Otherwise, parenting can become a meandering mess where you respond to whatever random stimuli happen to affect you moment by moment.

Our family's bull's-eye reads like this: *Train and launch L3 warriors who make a dent where they're sent.* We tried to make it short and easy to memorize—and uniquely personal to our family. We will unpack each part of this statement in the coming chapters. We'll also introduce the four stages of parenting:

- discipline stage (ages one to five)
- training stage (ages five to twelve)
- coaching stage (ages twelve to eighteen)
- friendship stage (ages eighteen plus)

When it comes to legacy, we can either continue a great one or change a bad one. I am so grateful to Jesus for allowing us the chance to change the future of the Wilson name.

It is *never* too late.

CHAPTER 4

BREAKING DOWN THE *Bull's-Eye*

At the end of the last chapter, we shared our family's bull's-eye: *Train and launch L3 warriors who make a dent where they're sent.* Here is a breakdown of what this meant to us.

TRAIN

It may not be the most popular word in our modern world, where parents undertake every role in their kids' lives—from coach to mentor to friend (and each of these has its place)—but God has called us as parents to train our children as we "bring them up in the discipline and instruction of the Lord" (Ephesians 6:4 ESV).

People often tend to either be afraid of the word *discipline* or overeager to use it as a tool for fearmongering and dominance. The biblical balance is somewhere in between, but it is always about "bring them up."

Yes, you are in charge of disciplining your kids, but the first part of this verse reminds us to know that God does not intend for your kids to be raised in a military-like environment. Ephesians 6:4 reveals God's heart that we remain as relationally aligned to our kids as possible, even when we must discipline them: "Fathers, do not exasperate your children." This doesn't mean we are supposed to be their best friends who never correct them either. That won't help them to grow into the adults they must become.

But the goal should be that your kids think of you as a safe place—the kind of people who may actually become their friends somewhere down the road. So if you find yourself invoking the almighty "because I said so, that's why!" more than anything else you say, you may be inching toward that steep face of discipline that can lead your kids to resent the very authority they should be able to respect and trust, even if they don't always like it. Yes, there are times to put your foot down, but if your foot never moves from that position, you may be inadvertently squashing someone underneath. Dictators don't care whether or not their subjects are angry or frustrated over their decrees or methods, but wise parents will at least pay attention to the feeling in their homes and avoid provoking such unresolved anger.

Again, the second half of the verse says it best: "bring them up" with your discipline and instruction. That's the goal: never to push them down, but always to bring them up. This will involve training them in all the ways the circumstances of life will require, including discipline.

To be clear, it is not our church's job or the school's job to train our kids. It is *our* job, and it is a privilege, even though it is hard and never-ending. When you train to run a marathon, not that we've ever done so, it requires a daily schedule that prepares you to accomplish this goal—you can't just run a few miles the week before and then set off thinking you can reach 26.2 miles.

Parenting is the same. Once you know what you're shooting for, you can develop a training regimen that aims to help you get closer to that specific target over time.

I remember walking into the kitchen one day and hearing Ann on the phone with Austin, who was driving back to college. Ann said, "Okay, I'll call AAA and have them out to your car in a few minutes to change that tire." I immediately realized that Austin was on the side of the road with a flat tire and had called home to see what to do.

I, Daddy "Tight Wad," grabbed the phone and said, "Hey, Austin, Dad here. We are not going to send AAA out there to fix your tire. *You* are going to change that tire." He said, "I don't know how." And I said, "I know because I never trained you. But I'm going to train you right now!" So, over the phone, I walked him through finding the spare tire in the trunk and putting that baby on the car. It took over an hour, but when we were done, Austin was ecstatic that he had changed his own tire. And the best part is that it didn't cost me a dime!

Knowing how to change a tire isn't one of life's most important skills, but I realized in that moment that I had failed to train my son in a simple skill he can use for the rest of his life. Immediately after I hung up the phone (and gave Ann a smirk that said, "Yes, I am an All-World Dad), I yelled, "Hey, Cody, let's go out to the driveway and change the tire on your car." He didn't need a new tire, but I realized that part of my job is to train my sons in life skills, and I could seize the opportunity at that moment rather than wait for difficulty to surface.

Ann was a master at this in the way she trained our boys in relationships. When one of them would become angry, she wouldn't just say, "Quit being angry!" Rather, she would walk them through why they were angry and how to process that anger. I would hear her training the boys by saying, "You are going to need to know how to work through your anger and hurt someday in your marriage or at work, so let's walk through your feelings right now and express them in a healthy way." Truth be told, she did a lot of relationship training with me as well.

Our kids are only under our roof for a short time, so we need to grab moments each and every day to train them on the most important life skills they will soon apply in adulthood.

LAUNCH

An arrow is not created to merely sit in a quiver for a lifetime. An arrow is made to be shot at a specific target. As hard as it can be to stomach the idea, we should become comfortable—and even joyful—with the truth that God has given us children who have a purpose to go away at some point to fulfill God's call on their lives. We would love to have all of our sons still living in our home, but besides the free rent, we doubt their wives would appreciate it very much! God called them out of our home to go build their own homes and raise the next generation in their families toward a similar bull's-eye. God did not call us to launch boomerangs.

We both cried as we dropped each of our sons off at college. We drove away with tears in our eyes and looked in the rearview mirror, knowing that the future would look much different than the past. We were scared too. Had we prepared them well for the world they were about to face? Yet the cause of our fear and sadness was exactly what God had called us to do as parents. We had trained them, and it was now time to launch them to their future.

As hard as it may be, remembering this future purpose

as the primary ring around your bull's-eye can sustain you through difficult moments when it feels like the world is closing in around you—when a childish behavior or hang-up seems like it will never be resolved. You can begin getting your own version of parental cabin fever while living through one of your kids' difficult stages. It can feel as if things will never change.

But remember this: they will change, whether you want them to or not. Aim not just for the present, but also for the future. Stay the course and realize that the moment you are in, even when it feels like an eternity, will not last forever. There are things that *do* last forever, so keep your eyes focused on them . . . even when your eyes are going cross out of frustration or involuntarily shut out of exhaustion.

This "launch moment" is both joyful and terrifying for a parent. I can still see the look on the faces of all three of our sons as they walked out of the chapel with their new brides after each of their weddings. Each had an expression of excitement as they faced their future with pure, unbridled confidence. Ann and I looked at each other and smiled in a way that clearly communicated our shared thought without having to verbalize it: *they have no clue what's coming.*

L3

L3 is a reference to the core values of the church we helped plant as cofounders more than thirty years ago. At Kensington Church, we developed three core values that reflected what we hoped every member would eventually become. The three Ls were *Love*, *Lock*, and *Live*. We called them L3 just to make it easier to remember. These simply mean that a follower of Jesus is a disciple who:

- loves God and others
- locks arms in community
- lives openhandedly

As a family, we decided that L3 accurately expressed what God desires a follower of Jesus to look like, so we adopted these as goals for raising our sons. We hoped and prayed that when they were men, they would love God with all their heart, soul, mind, and strength because they would come to realize how much God first loves them. (This key of God's first love for them was something they would first experience—or not experience—from us, their parents.) Then from an overflow of this overwhelming love for them, they would love others as they love themselves and as they have been loved by Christ.

We also prayed that they would intentionally find a community of other Christ followers with whom they would lock arms, serve together, and raise families together, just as we had done with our community. Proverbs 18:1 (ESV) makes clear the dangers of walking alone: "Whoever isolates himself seeks his own desire; he breaks out against all sound judgment." You don't want to deal day in and day out with the challenges in your home without people close to you who encourage you and give you the perspective you don't always have when you're so close to the situation. Fatigue, anxiety, stress, and everything that can come along with real life as a parent will most definitely cloud your parental judgment.

And by "most definitely," we mean it *will* happen to you—like the actual you, not just everyone else reading this book... like really. Scripture doesn't pull any punches here: to go it alone in any part of life, including parenting, is to seek your own way and to take up arms against good judgment. You want good judgment on your side, not the other way around, so you have to get others on your side who will continually and intentionally help you find it. Good judgment and good community go hand in hand. Some of the greatest gifts God has given us are the couples and families with whom we do life and with whom we have raised our kids. It has also been a gift that we have intentionally pursued. Our hope has always been that when they became husbands and dads, our sons would also choose to do life with others. And that's exactly what they've chosen to do.

Finally, we prayed that our sons would be generous. We wanted them to learn to live with open hands and bless others. Generosity includes money, but it doesn't stop there. Finding out what we're created to do and then investing ourselves wholeheartedly in others is what it means to live openhandedly.

God's ways lead us to look up first, outward second, and inward last. This is the opposite of the way we are wired. The natural bent of the human heart is toward selfishness. To live openhandedly, we must surrender our hearts to Jesus and allow him to transform us. In order for our kids to see what that looks like, they need to see it modeled by us as their parents. They are watching us 24-7, and whether we like it or not, they will most likely emulate what they see. It's scary, but it's the truth.

Grace allows us to look in the mirror as parents without being crushed by what we're not doing perfectly. That is how we grow authentically—because you can't give away what you don't first possess. And you can't begin to humbly gain what you can't admit you don't have.

Maybe it's time to hit your knees (as the first of much more knee-hitting to come) and ask God to produce in you what you are hoping he will produce in your children. Seriously, go ahead and do it right now. We'll wait . . .

WARRIORS

This one brings up something every parent feels but often struggles to articulate. Raising kids doesn't just feel like a battle; it actually *is* a battle. We must never forget that from a spiritual standpoint, we are living in a war zone. We're talking not about a physical war against a hostile organization or country but about a spiritual war that is invisible, yet more real than what you can see with your eyes (see Ephesians 6:10–12).

There is an enemy of our souls who is also the enemy of the souls of our kids. His name is Satan—and he hates you and your children. He doesn't have mercy on little ones, but rather, like the coward he is, he seeks them out as easier prey. His goal is to destroy all that God is building, so he will attack your home and family because God is greatly at work in those places.

But God is building warriors who will go to battle to advance his kingdom. As parents, we get to watch and serve God as he builds stable, able warriors for this kingdom. This is why setting the goal that our kids simply become happy adults someday is not enough. Of course, we truly hope your kids and our kids become happy as they continue to grow, but more importantly, we hope they understand that their lives matter for eternal things—and that how they live can either support or help destroy the darkness. As adults, we hope they wake up each day and pray, "God, how do you want to use me today? How can I serve you to reveal your love and grace to someone else? Please use me today to advance your kingdom."

This is a target worth shooting at, so don't settle for anything less.

MAKE A DENT WHERE THEY ARE SENT

"Make a dent where they are sent" is a phrase we've often used when preaching at our church. We strongly believe that God has strategically placed each one of us to be his light. Jesus said it best when he told his disciples:

> "You are the light of the world. A town built on a hill cannot be hidden. Neither do people light a lamp and put it under a bowl. Instead they put it on its stand, and it gives light to everyone in the house. In the same way, let your light shine before others, that they may see your good deeds and glorify your Father in heaven."
>
> *Matthew 5:14–16*

Jesus was giving his disciples a bull's-eye to shoot for with their lives. It gets better though. The original language of the words "town built on a hill" specifically referred to a town strategically placed that could not be hidden. Jesus was teaching his disciples then—as well as his disciples now—an important truth. Just as a city in those days was strategically placed in a location where others could see it and find it when they were looking for safety and help, we too are strategically placed by God to bring safety and help to those around us who are seeking the same.

Our lives are not simply random. God wants to use us where he has placed us to advance his kingdom. *Make a dent where we are sent.* Be and give hope for those who hurt, comfort for those who mourn, food for those who hunger, shelter for those who shiver in the cold, and more.

The question most people want to ask is, "Okay, then, where am I sent?" The answer is profound in its simplicity: *you are sent where you are.* The job you have, the house or apartment or condo where you're living, the school you're attending, the sports team your kid is playing on—*these* are where God has strategically placed you right now. Make a difference where you are planted. Make a dent for Jesus.

I was a coach on all three of our sons' football teams from their Pee Wee leagues up through high school. It was one way I chose to be a part of their lives. After our high school games on Friday nights, the coaching staff usually headed to a local pub to talk about the game. As a pastor, I felt that a bar wasn't the best place for me to be seen with my coaching buddies, and yet I knew that God had called me to make a dent where I was being sent—which meant he had sent me to do life with these coaches and their families.

One Friday night after a victory, I called my buddy Rob, a fellow believer on the coaching staff, and said, "We need to be at the bar with the coaches." He agreed, and off we went to drink our Cokes with the guys. When we walked into the bar, the coaches stood up and gave us a standing ovation. They were *that* excited we had joined them.

I sat next to our special teams coach, Jack. He asked me why I never cussed while coaching the team. Not cussing may be a little thing that doesn't make me more righteous than anyone else, but regardless, it gave me the chance to share how Jesus changes all parts of a person's life. I told him how I had gone from being a man with a foul mouth to the person I was in the present only because of Jesus.

This was the first of many conversations with Jack that led to more questions about faith. A few months later, Jack surrendered his life to Christ. Along with his wife and kids, Jack now serves at our church. God began this change in Jack by leading me to hang with him at the local bar.

God wants to use you and your children right where he has planted you. There is truly no higher calling than to be able to pass on such a vision to your kids in a way that is life-changing for them and for you.

MAKING THE MOST OF YOUR OPPORTUNITIES

As parents, we're old enough to know that the things of this world cannot truly make one happy. We have the opportunity to impart to our children a grander vision for their lives—one that involves more than just what the world says will make them happy. We get to aim their lives toward the right target, training them to be confident that God wants to use their unique wiring, disposition, location, talents, communities, and experiences to advance the kingdom of God wherever he sends them.

Many think God only calls and sends full-time Christian missionaries and pastors, but the truth is, we are *all* full-time missionaries. He has sent each of us to shine and make a dent where we are. This is not motivational, evangelistic rhetoric. This is the essence of God's calling on our lives. God has a mission of reaching the world with his love and grace through Jesus. Parents get to train L3 warriors for that mission. They live in our homes only for a season before they launch. What a privilege, but also what a responsibility!

If we understand this epic mission we have as parents, it changes everything, doesn't it? Having a bull's-eye like this brings purpose and direction to what can often become a daily grind as a parent. Take it from one of us (we'll let you guess which one). You are *not* going to be thinking about this target when your kid begins peeing on your forehead. Nor will it be in the forefront of your mind when your dog eats all of the Christmas chocolate and pukes into the heater vents, causing the entire house to smell like chocolate puke for the holidays. (What a sweet fragrance that was!) The target probably *won't* be in your mind when you're late to another parent-teacher meeting, soccer practice, or the thousand other challenges that come along with being a parent.

Even if you don't always look at it every moment, the target should always be there to return to. It is stationary when everything else swirls around you like a tornado. It will guide you—and guide you back—each step of this long, beautiful journey.

One of the strategies we incorporated to help us move toward our bull's-eye was placing a family night on our calendar every Friday. This became a ritual our boys looked forward to each week, and they were convinced every family did the same thing. Ann and I had different family experiences growing up. Ann came from a more stable environment, while the story you've already heard from me (Dave) lets you know I came from a family that never once hosted a planned gathering. Regardless, we had the opportunity to create strategies for aiming our kids at our own family target, which was something that would hopefully shift our legacy toward a new one.

We gave our evening a name: Wilson Party Night. We also made up a song to sing as we began the evening. We would pick up the boys from grade school on Friday afternoon and drive straight to the movie store to rent a VHS movie. If you don't know what VHS stands for, you can check out old examples in the Smithsonian Museum . . . or just google it. As we drove to the movie store, we'd sing our Party Night song:

Party night, party night!
Party night at the Wilson home!

We'll be there.
We'll be square.
We'll be wearing our underwear!

We would laugh all the way home. Now I (Dave) have to tell you that this laughter was a direct overflow of Ann's personality. She wanted to have a home full of joy and fun. And man oh man, did she create just that. Once when the boys were little, I was taking a shower, and the boys came running into the bathroom with a bucket full of ice water that they threw on me. They ran out of the room laughing hysterically. They may have done the actual ice dumping, but I knew who the mastermind really was. This was just another case of Ann creating a house full of joy. Daily pranks and ice-cold showers were commonplace.

So for us, Wilson Party Night was an extension of creating a home full of joy that the boys would want to bring their friends to, especially during their future teen years. As we got home from the movie store, we would throw big pillows and blankets on the family room floor in front of our huge nineteen-inch TV, which had vise grips connected to the TV knobs as the channel changer (not kidding). After everyone threw on their jammies, we would watch a great kid-friendly movie while eating real popcorn—none of that microwave imposter popcorn on party night!

Cody would usually fall asleep before the movie was finished, while CJ and Austin would fight us to stay up late, which we usually allowed. Once we got the boys down for the night, we would head back down together to the family room, where all those comfy pillows and blankets still lay strewn across the floor.

I (Dave) would usually give Ann "the look" and say, "What do you think?"

And I (Ann) would usually offer a certain look back in

his direction that gently communicated without words, *Are you kidding me? Do you even know what I've done all day as a mom?*

But every once in a while, I (Ann) would wink back at him, and you know what that meant . . . one of the kids was about to wake up crying. Like clockwork.

Those fun times created the atmosphere we wanted our kids to remember. Yes, it was a part of the training—the part where trust, fun, and love abounded.

Wherever you are, pull out a sheet of paper right now. You can also use your phone or computer. It doesn't matter how you begin the process, as long as you begin somewhere. Start writing a bull's-eye for your family. It needs to be a reflection of God's ultimate goals for your family legacy. Dream big, not small. Be specific, and make sure everything you write reflects a biblical concept. You can use ours as a reference, but try to make your own.

Trust us, if you don't write it down, it won't happen. So start right now, and then begin praying that God will help you put it into action.

— Reflections —

THIRD SON: CODY

- My mom is one of the most encouraging people I've ever known. If you have ever been the server for our family at a restaurant, I'm sure she has complimented you. My mom has a habit of finding the good in people and encouraging them. You can see people's days change as she speaks life into them. I've witnessed people's lives changed because she believes in them more than they believe in themselves.

- I believe my mom embodies Jesus' ability to see greatness where others see outcasts and failures. Would your kids say you believe in them more than they believe in themselves? Would your kids say, "My parents see greatness in me, even when all I see is failure"?
- When I was younger, my mom would always tell me I was a leader. But when she told me this, I didn't always feel encouraged, I felt pressure. In my mind, I was not a leader. I felt like she really didn't know me and that I couldn't live up to that title. The idea of leading was a daunting and fearful thought. As I reflect back on those words now, I understand my mom wasn't calling me to be something; she was reminding me of who I always was. As parents, we need to remind our kids of who they are, not just tell them what to do.
- When I was in high school, I didn't know who I was. When you don't know *who you are*, you become *where you are*. I became like the people I hung out with because that was the version of me people seemed to love. I was a chameleon. So when my mom spoke life into me and expressed her pride, I once again thought she was wrong about who I was. If she really knew me, she would know I was fake, a failure, a hypocrite, and that I wasn't enough. I now understand that my mom was reminding me of what I forgot: who I truly was. She wasn't telling me who I could be; she was reminding me of who I was always created to be.
- As I look back on my life, I remember my mom's words of encouragement more than any discipline. I remember the letter my dad wrote me during my freshman year at college, reminding me that I have what it takes. (I think my mom made him write it—haha.) I remember them hugging me after my first time preaching and celebrating who I was. This is what I remember most.
- I'll be honest, I still don't know the exact line or mark my parents were aiming at with my life. I learned what it was as I read this

book, just like you. With that said, I believe the aiming point isn't who your kids might be some day; it's who God has already created them to be. Don't shape them into who you want them to be, but rather call out who God has created them to be. Hold that vision for their life, and continually remind them of who they are.

- I can imagine a gardener watering a small apple seed and saying, "One day you'll be a mighty tree that gives food and life to others." All of the potential of a mighty tree is in that seed. The seed just needs love, care, and devotion to become mighty and life-giving. Today maybe your kids are just in seed form. Maybe you see no greatness, but take heart—all of the potential for something mighty is already inside them. Hold the vision of a mighty tree over their lives when they are in seed form. Water and care for them so they'll grow mighty and strong. Let your words of kindness and encouragement unlock them to grow. If your kids became the words you called them, who would they become?

PREPARING FOR THE STAGES OF PARENTING

By now, you have hopefully come to accept the indisputable fact that we (Dave and Ann) are *far* from perfect parents and our kids are far from perfect children. But our hope, and your hope, lies in the fact that God can overcome the many imperfections that result from missing targets in our own lives as parents (also known as our sin) and empower us to keep working in our families in ways we never could all on our own.

That's why we continue to surrender our children to him, prayerfully hoping he will make something great happen in spite of our constant failings as parents. This means you can do the same—and that you can also give yourself some grace. You're not going to get this one perfect, so grace is necessary to know how to approach each day's challenges. It is all too easy to beat ourselves up for the many ways we fail as parents.

Most of the time, we don't have a clue what we're doing—and if we think we do, there's a good chance we're doing it wrong anyway. We need God to intervene and fix what we've broken. It was nearly a daily occurrence for both of us to do something wrong or say something we regretted, which was followed by a grim image of our grown child lying on a counselor's couch, "unpacking" the enormous, duffle-sized amount of baggage that his messed-up parents dumped on him.

In our minds, we were messing up his life . . . forever!

Be reminded by two parents who didn't get it right that forever is not only a very long time but also an arena of time we're not in charge of. Not to be cliché, but forever is God's business. As we begin to delve into the stages of parenting and all the practical applications that accompany them, always remember that these are tools, not assurances or guarantees. The grace of God that secures our forever—and the forevers of our kids—is the only assurance we really have in this life.

It's also the only one we really need. It holds steady when all else gives way.

In the next several chapters, we want to focus on the various stages of parenting. Every stage is different, so just when you think you have this whole parenting thing down, it all changes on you. Even so, there are principles and insights that can help you either navigate with more health the stage you're in or better prepare your expectations for the stage to come.

Thirty-four years ago, I (Dave) remember bringing CJ home from the hospital, putting him in the crib, and just looking at him and thinking, *Okay, now what?* Where was the owner's manual for this new person we were supposed to keep alive? I honestly had no clue what to do—and that's not an exaggeration.

But there actually is an owner's manual for parenting and it's as close as your phone. The Bible is a complex work that spans thousands of years of history across varying cultures and cultural interpretations. We believe it is inspired by God and that every word in it is not only helpful but also transformative for a full and fulfilling life.

This does not mean you can just open it up, find a random verse, and "go and do likewise." Many things in the Bible are not for us in our time—things like animal sacrifices, weeklong feasts (which sounds amazing), weeklong fasts (which sounds not so amazing), annual pilgrimages, the management of mildew in one's tent, and much more. Many people today seem to miss the context of Scripture and where we fall into it. This causes them to cherry-pick certain things from the Bible that jibe with what they like and to simply overlook the other, less comfortable parts.

Understanding where we fall in the timeline of eternity and how this affects the application of Scripture is one of the keys to gaining a fuller, healthier understanding of all the ways Scripture enriches our lives today. After all, God's words are both alive and active in transforming our lives. We shouldn't try to boil them down to their base, bumper-sticker versions as if we're quoting our favorite author or comic strip. God's Word is complex—yet rightly applied in context, Scripture and the principles derived from it can become to us that very "owner's manual" we so often feel we're lacking in our parental journeys.

It doesn't give you every specific for the modern life, but it does remind you of and instruct you in what's truly important in all of life, ancient or modern. Will the Bible tell you what to do when a kid pees in your face? Not specifically. But will God's words reveal the correct posture for loving, leading, and disciplining your children in a way that actually works? Every single time.

That's why it is important to base your parenting targets, as well as your parenting adjustments when the targets are missed, on Scripture. When the only option that seems doable is to bear down and put the entire household into a collective, rage-filled headlock, Scripture will remind you, "A person's wisdom yields *patience*; it is to one's glory to overlook an offense" (Proverbs 19:11, emphasis ours). God's words will continually remind you where life is found, thus keeping you from inadvertently seeking life in less than desirable places, where it doesn't exist anyway.

We tend to beat ourselves up as parents if our kids are making bad choices in their teen years. To the defense of parents everywhere, all teens will probably do some bonehead things because all teens' brains aren't fully developed yet. I (Dave) guarantee that my single mom was seriously wondering what I would turn into the night she had to bail me out of jail for getting caught mooning another car on I-75! She screamed at me during the entire ride home, telling me I was headed toward destruction if I didn't wise up. It was a fun ride home. But look at me now—I haven't mooned anyone (publicly) in more than fifty years.

Some may call that a no-streaking streak.

Your kids will "expose" you to many of their own unique challenges at every stage of their development, not just in their teen years. Aiming at the right target in your parenting is not about foreseeing and preparing to handle everything they could do wrong—this will drive you and them crazy. The right target of parenting is much simpler, even when parenting itself is complicated. It's about trusting God to work powerfully as he brings about his plan in our kids' lives, especially when we lose hope in our own plans.

Do not judge your value as a parent while your kid is a teen—hear us, your judgment won't be accurate. If you decide to evaluate yourself, try doing so when they've reached thirty—or now that we have a thirty-four-year-old, maybe wait until they're forty. The point is, as you explore these seasons of parenting, keep a grace-first mindset that affords some elasticity to their stages and to your performance as a parent. Flexibility in thought, plan, and action will be one of your greatest assets.

Let's revisit the four stages of parenting:

- discipline stage (ages one to five)
- training stage (ages five to twelve)
- coaching stage (ages twelve to eighteen)
- friendship stage (ages eighteen plus)

Obviously, these stages will overlap sometimes, as will our parenting strategies. Even so, understanding these different seasons can help give us direction—or perhaps just a life raft—for navigating whatever unique season we find ourselves paddling through. Let's begin with the first stage—the discipline stage (ages one to five).

CHAPTER 5

WALKING THROUGH THE *Valley of the Shadow*

Discipline Stage, Ages One to Five

KICKING MAD

Guilt.

It was my (Ann's) new companion, nestled comfortably between my two shoulder blades. Weighty. Hefty. Sometimes it took my breath away as I clomped through the early years of being a mom. Where did this heavy backpack of burden come from? I had never before wrestled with the weight of it to this extent. It had become my ever-present luggage—a weight I never welcomed and never anticipated would so severely hinder my movements as a mom.

But it did.

It seemed heavier at night when I collapsed into bed after herding three small boys through a seemingly endless day. *They* were my joy and delight, so it was clear that *I* was the problem. I seemed to become consistently agitated, irritated, impatient, and frustrated. And on this day, I had secured the title of The Ultimate Failure as a Mom (trademark pending).

The day was typical, starting off with high hopes and enthusiasm. I was ready to tackle whatever lay ahead. *Bring it on world . . . I'm ready to rumble!*

Dave had a busy day ahead of him too, so he was already off to work before any of us had awakened. Breakfast eaten, kitchen cleaned, lunches packed, all three boys in the car, and we were off to school. I patted myself on the back, feeling accomplished and confident. My part-time job held a few responsibilities, and I would have our four-year-old Cody with me for the day. Even so, this day held a world of promise and possibilities.

"Jesus, thank you for a new day, and that Christmas is right around the corner," I prayed aloud as we drove to school. The mention of Christmas brought all three of my passengers in the car to rapt attention. "Help us all to be a light today for you wherever we go and in whatever we do. Help CJ and Austin at school today—may they feel your closeness and your love, and help Cody and me to get done what we need to do today. In Jesus' name. Amen."

I had engaged in praying with my kids, which guaranteed that things would go well. Right?

"Love you guys! Have fun today. Bye!" And they were off.

Thursday morning was in the books, and the normally heavy companion between my shoulders actually felt light and seemingly unnoticed. *Heck, I've finally got this mom thing down,* I proudly thought as I congratulated myself on the high quality of my mothering skills. The day trudged on uneventfully, a welcome rarity in a mom's life. Job wrapped up for the day. Grocery shopping accomplished. Calls made. Lists checked off. Kids home from school. Dinner made. Children fed. All the boxes checked.

Hmm, where is Dave? I thought he'd be home by now. I thought his meeting was supposed to be done hours ago.

Horseplay and roughhousing had begun to ramp up in the family room. It was getting loud. The weight began to be slightly felt—and its timing was eerily familiar. This was the part of the day when frenzy and craziness would often envelope the house in a crescendo that was sure to end with someone getting hurt and tears . . .

The kids sometimes cried too.

I actually found this time of the day to be fun—well, most of the time. With nine-, seven-, and four-year-old boys in the house, *calm* and *quiet* were not adjectives we used much. It was like a roller-coaster ride where the next dip promised to be exhilarating—or cause you to throw up on all the other passengers.

Where is Dave? I looked at the clock again. I was getting irritated this time. I didn't want him to miss these family moments, but more truthfully, I needed his help in all the corralling that needed to be done to get these young stallions herded into the shower and bed.

"CJ, we need to practice your spelling words for your test tomorrow. Let's go to the kitchen to do it away from the distractions."

Distractions? More like complete and utter mayhem, I thought to myself as a pillow was hurled at CJ's head. The pillow was a timely reminder to him that he was about to miss out on the fun. He and I trudged into the kitchen for boring spelling words. Ugh, I didn't want to go either. CJ slumped at the table, pulled the list out of his backpack, and began to look over the words as I started cleaning up the kitchen from the dinner.

Where is Dave?

For the next thirty minutes, CJ and I went over each word with painstaking slowness. He was distracted by everything, while I was distracted by Dave's absence. Officially, I was starting to get mad. *He should have been home hours ago. Why hasn't he called? Why am I doing this all by myself yet again?*

I looked over at CJ. What a great kid! He was so fun and easy to be around. His highly intelligent mind was always working, but he hated the monotony of school and homework. His teacher had commented that he was easily distracted and mentioned the possibility of ADHD. I pondered the possibility as I searched his face. He was trying to knock the saltshaker over with the edge of his eraser. We had been on the same dumb spelling word for fifteen minutes. This was not going well.

Where is Dave?

Yelling and tears both erupted in the family room as Austin and Cody were fighting like Spartans and Athenians over a solitary toy—the coveted object of ill repute. Someone was pinched or punched or gouged or something of the sort, and now they were both yelling for me to play the role of referee—or better to say, geopolitical diplomat.

CJ was unfocused, so I tried to stay focused on the task at hand. "CJ, come on. Pay attention! Let's get this word right this time. How do you spell ______?

Just as the question had left my lips, his eraser achieved success and the saltshaker tipped over, spilling salt all over the table.

That's it! The screaming and salting and waiting and trying—it was suddenly all too much.

"Ohhhh myyyy goshhhhhh!" I yelled at the top of my lungs. And without thinking, I swung my leg back and kicked the wall as if I was David Beckham kicking the winning goal for the Olympic gold. The impact was surprisingly fierce as my little five-foot-one, 115-pound frame gave it everything I had.

My foot was successful in pounding a hefty hole in the kitchen wall. It was less successful in being retracted out of said hole; that is to say, it stayed there, stuck in the drywall.

You know how you often can't scream loud enough to get your kids to come to you? Well, like baby bears to a dumpster, my three suddenly attentive fans ran to where I was in the kitchen, watching my every move as I awkwardly tried to unhinge my foot from the broken array of drywall that had entrapped it in shame. Shock and astonishment radiated from their faces alongside fear and wonder, as if to say, *How could this miracle have been accomplished by our mere and mortal mom?*

I didn't look at CJ.

Austin looked up, searching my face, trying to decide whether he should laugh or be afraid. He chose the latter.

Cody's little four-year-old face looked at me with total wonder and admiration. He was impressed that I had kicked all the way through the wall, which was no doubt inspiring him to find ways to do the same.

Shame, guilt, fear, and horror began their treacherous group ascent to my mind, carrying with them ample supplies of accusations. Their cleated boots of unworthiness dug into my soul, piercing me with each step.

What kind of mom are you?

What kind of mom could lose her temper like that?

What will your kids remember about you?

What will this do to mess up your kids?

You are a failure!

I heard it over and over in my head. The backpack I thought I had finally mastered was suddenly full of bricks again, heavier than ever.

I felt a sense of panic as I quickly realized that Dave, my husband (and my pastor), would be walking through the door at any minute. *What would I tell him?* My mind was racing when a brilliant thought surged through the middle of the pack. I sprinted up the stairs two at a time, racing into my closet, eyes searching for the box of leftover wallpaper. *Yes!* I foraged through the box, finding my prize, and sprinted back down the stairs, only to find three sets of innocent eyes peering thoughtfully into the eight-inch cavern of broken drywall.

Whipping the scissors out of the kitchen drawer, I commanded my now coconspirators to step aside as I began to cover up the crime scene before "Pastor Dave" walked in the door. This was working perfectly! No one would ever know until wallpaper went out of style, and hopefully I'd be in a new house by then. Besides, even if it were to go out of style, Dave would be the last to notice. Ah, the cunning mind of a mother!

A cut here, a matching flower there, a little water, and *voila*, job completed. Reputation intact. My mothering skills might have been waning, but my wallpaper skills were on point. Dave would never know. *I mean, maybe I should tell him, but why burden him with my issues when he has so many more worthy things to worry about? I could ask the boys to not tell him, but would that be taking this too far?*

I had already gone too far, but I didn't know it. As I was contemplating my next move in the whole diabolical cover-up, the sound of the garage door suddenly interrupted my thought patterns, and in came Dave like "Dad of the Year."

"Dad!" All three boys rushed to him with glee. They were so excited to see him. Maybe they would forget to tell him about the maniac wall crusher they once called Mom. After all, their attention spans were notoriously short—heck, they would literally forget their shoes in the rain on any given day. Or to wipe. Or to eat. They literally forgot everything we had ever asked them to remember!

But alas, they had not forgotten this. *Cruel irony* is an insufficient description.

I couldn't be angry with him—he was only four years old.

Sure enough, Cody was the rat . . . an adorable loose end I hadn't had the heart to tie up. "Dad, you won't believe what happened tonight!" He still retained that same look of wonder and admiration—it was a blaring spotlight that refused to let me hide. "Mom is wayyyyy stronger than we thought!"

"What do you mean?" Dave looked questionably at me, innocent curiosity twinkling in his eyes. I could feel my face redden with shame.

Then like a perfectly trained musical trio, all three boys blurted out the truth in simultaneous, harmonious merriment: "Mom kicked a hole in the wall!" Fine time they picked to suddenly be on the same page in brotherly unity.

BACKPACKS APLENTY

I will spare you the boring details of my pathetic explanation to Dave. The bottom line was that I felt intense guilt and shame over the whole ordeal. They took giant chisels and began wreaking havoc on my soul like the carvings of Mount Rushmore, except what was resulting from their blunt-force work wasn't producing something beautiful or majestic. It was ugly, as if all the presidents were somehow scolding me with their icy eyes of condemnation.

George Washington's fixed gaze of disappointment is harsher than you think.

I had already profusely apologized to CJ multiple times over, reminding him that my anger and wall kicking had nothing to do with him or that dumb spelling word. I reminded him that he was super smart and wonderful. I also apologized to Austin and Cody, reminding them that I had made a horrible mistake that had nothing to do with them either. This was about *me* not exercising self-control and, in fact, being *out of control.* I asked for their forgiveness, which each quickly gave with no ill feelings—none that I could detect anyway. We prayed together, and they heard me ask God for forgiveness and to help me not lose my temper.

What had happened to me? Just for the record, before having children, I had never before in my life struggled with any sort of anger or temper issues. It wasn't even remotely normal for me to lose control of my faculties in any way. What had happened to me?

Maybe you've asked the same question, especially as the parent of littles. Maybe you pictured yourself as a gentle, protecting, fun-loving nurturer who would listen, respond with kindness, and ultimately guide these little offshoots of your own life into safe places. Male or female, I think we all hold newborns in our arms and in that moment cannot imagine ever losing our tempers or engaging in patterns of harshness toward someone so lovely, innocent, and helpless.

This cosmic bond to our children is a beautiful, God-created feature of parenthood. It prepares our hearts for fierce devotion, endurance through sleepless nights, and an undying tenacity to keep going no matter what happens. But our hearts can twist this beautiful feeling into unrealistically high expectations for ourselves—lofty imaginations that our actions will always perfectly match the breathtaking intensity of the love we feel in those early moments.

So when we mess up, when we kick walls, when we yell at our precious ones with words that aren't so precious, our expectations meet a reality we never thought would find us. It happens to moms and dads all the time, and it certainly happened to me on a regular basis.

How many nights had I already gone to bed feeling like a

failure as a mom? Too many to count. I often couldn't sleep because the weight of my guilt was stealing my breath away. I often thought of the many single moms and dads who were raising their kids without the help of a spouse or partner. They were the real heroes. They should get trophies every day of their parenting lives. Here I was doing this with a loving husband in a thriving community with all of my physical needs being met—and yet I just couldn't seem to get it all together. I experienced a newfound admiration for Dave's mom, who had raised him by herself... and I bet she never kicked a hole in one of their walls.

I recall a friend of mine who seemed shocked when I told her that I sometimes yelled at our boys because they were driving me crazy. Her look of shock and condemnation toward me only stirred up more guilt and shame.

"What, you've never yelled at your kids?" I asked accusingly.

"No!" she resolutely replied. Ugh—my backpack of shame and guilt took on a hefty extra twenty pounds after that particular conversation.

You see, the backpacks we carry as parents are even heavier nowadays than they were when I was raising young children. After all, these are the days of multiple social media platforms as our chief modus operandi of communicating with the world. You post pictures of your airbrushed kids (well, I guess technically it's the picture that's airbrushed, not the kids—unless things get really interesting). You write your lovely post about them with a few pithy hashtags while I like your post and counter with a post of my own. This is the common method for the information we gather, even if only subconsciously, about all the other parents around us.

This method most certainly causes mothers and fathers to fall into the trap of comparison, which also produces feelings of doubt, inadequacy, and failure. When we are inundated with pictures and cutesy quips of a million anecdotes and accomplishments of others' remarkable children, we suddenly feel that our experience as parents is somehow less than remarkable—maybe just "markable," I suppose.

I've been there—in fact, I've *lived there* far too long. The good news is, you don't have to. Let me share what has taken thirty-five years of parenting to discover and what I wish I would have known and lived out back then: *you are enough*.

I know we've already told you this once before in the early chapters, but it bears repeating here. You see, you are enough because Jesus has personally assigned you to raise this child (or children). You are exactly who your kids, foster kids, adopted kids, prodigal kids, and hurting kids need. I know it may feel as if they need someone better who won't kick in the walls (and you probably shouldn't make a habit of doing so, even if only for the sake of your contractor), but you are the one they really need the most.

Moms and dads, know this: you are going to fail, but this *doesn't* mean you are a failure as a parent or as a person. And your kids are going to fail too. This doesn't mean that who they are as people is unredeemable. Shame leads us to believe we are flawed beyond repair, and thus unworthy of love or belonging. While guilt precipitates the question, "What have I done?" shame causes us to ask, "Who am I to do such things?" In other words, shame leads us to internalize conclusions about our character and nature, not just our actions.

Shame is the heaviest brick in the backpack of parenting—and once it is picked up, it is not easily unloaded. The longer we walk with it, the more we tend to believe we are broken beyond healing. Just as it is hard to carry a heavy bag while lugging multiple children in car seats, the backpack of shame weighs us down and affects our parenting in negative ways we usually can't see in the moment. We tend to somehow think that carrying such shame is our noble penance, but it's really just extra weight holding us down—and threatening to hold our children back.

But failures don't have to be carried as if they are somehow parts of our being. We can confess, ask for forgiveness, make amends, and lay down the weight. Instead of making our failures into little masters who ride on our backs, we can learn from them as they fade into the distance behind us. After all, we're moving on—away from them.

I'm happy to report that I've never kicked a hole in a wall again. Have I made mistakes? There aren't enough pages to list them all. But I have become so thankful for God's sweet grace and do-overs. My worth as a parent is no longer determined by my stellar (or less than stellar) performance any given day as a parent—that bag was *way* too heavy to carry, even for someone as strong as me (just ask Cody).

Laying down these weights lets you be present in your home in the moments when your presence is most meaningful to your little ones. In fact, your presence combined with God's presence is the "it factor" in your home. It's the dynamic duo! It allows you to accept God's love for you, as well as reflect this love for your kids. In both cases, love covers over a host of sins.

God didn't wait for our perfection before he thought we were worthy of love or rescue. Instead, "God demonstrates his own love for us in this: While we were *still sinners*, Christ died for us" (Romans 5:8, emphasis mine). This is the sweetest reflection of parenting we can both receive and give. We know in our own children's lives that we don't wait for them to claw their way out of trouble or danger before running to them. No, *while* they are screaming in the grocery aisle, marking up their brother's face with a Sharpie, carving their name with a rock into the side of our minivan (true story), running toward the street, or any other number of possible yet average occurrences, we run to them immediately.

God runs to you too, even while you're making mistakes as a parent, so don't run from him. Accept grace when you need it the most and deserve it the least. This is what makes it grace in the first place.

This will also equip you to own up to your mistakes because you won't constantly be carrying them as if they are embedded in your very character. You will be able to trust in God's character rather than in your own. Doing so, by the way, is the only way your character can be transformed to look more like his. Grace leads to change, not condemnation or shame.

Again, it's important for our kids to see us own up to our mistakes, confess our sins, and ask Jesus to forgive us. When they see us authentically talking to God and hear us asking him for his power and his help, they become acutely (and also cutely) aware of their own need for Jesus too. This is the sweet spot already created for us in the gospel. Jesus redeems and forgives our mistakes from the past and present, and even the holes in the walls of our future. His blood covers our sin, just as my wallpaper covered the hole. This practice of talking to God as he is—that is, as a loving and forgiving Father—is crucial for our children to observe.

FROM BACKPACKS TO BATTLEFIELDS

Now back to the story. I'm embarrassed to tell you that after the kids were asleep and Dave had become gloriously comatose the instant his head hit the pillow (must be nice), I decided to get up and creep down the hallway. I needed to wake CJ up and once again tell him I was sorry. I thought doing so would help assuage the guilt and shame I felt. So that's what I did.

In fact, our boys will tell you I not only did so this one time, but time and time again when I felt I had wronged them. As they got older, I would write them letters of apology to remind them that I loved them and that my own poor decisions did not negate how amazing they were. I really thought that returning to this place of intense remorse would help unload my backpack of guilt and shame. It did not—after all, if it had, why did I feel the need to keep making amends for what had already been mended? The bottom line was that I didn't believe it had been mended. I wanted to keep helping, but I was only hurting myself and not fully trusting that God's grace was actually enough. I thought I wasn't enough, so that kept me from accepting that his grace was enough.

If I could go back and talk to young Ann, I would. But since I can't, I'll talk to you instead. I would tell her and you that Jesus died to rescue me not just from sin but also from the guilt and shame that result from it. You can't feel bad enough or work hard enough to remove them. Your kids or your spouse can't assure you it's okay enough times to remove them. Only Jesus can remove them, and the good news (literally, the Good News) is that he *wants* to remove them.

A spiritual battle is raging in every nook and cranny of your home. A thief seeks to ravage our homes and destroy every good thing God is doing there. The relationship we have with our kids is a sweet gift from God. We didn't create it, we don't deserve it, and our goodness doesn't maintain it. Likewise, if you are married, your spouse is a sweet gift from God. These gifts are the candy that Satan longs to take from God's babies—and it's very easy to do so if our understanding of grace remains in its infant stage. Satan will do anything in his power to destroy these relationships, because under our roofs is where warriors are being forged. Under our roofs is where disciples are being made. Under our roofs is where love is being learned and world changers are being birthed and launched.

Make no mistake, this feeling of constant guilt and shame may be reflective of your personality or it may not, but it is most certainly something your enemy longs to exploit. He seeks to fill up your backpack with weights. He wants to hinder you from experiencing the fullness of God's best intentions for your time with your kids. Through shame, the enemy robs you of joy in your present as you regret your past and fret over your future.

Love is God's undisputed champion in our homes—the true center of the bull's-eye. Satan will do anything in his power to distract us from this goal. Guilt and shame are some of his great maneuvers to try to move us to other targets. These can become crippling to parents, distracting us from seeing the good we're doing—and, more importantly, the good that *God* is doing regardless of our mistakes.

It can seem a little overdramatic to speak in terms like *enemy* and *battle*, but it is Jesus himself who portrayed these tensions in just such a way. He said, "The thief [Satan] comes only to steal and kill and destroy; I have come that they may have life, and have it to the full" (John 10:10). These are not passive terms. If someone were heading toward your home, and you knew their intention was to break in and steal, kill, and destroy what you hold most dear, you would take action—or at least you'd lock the door.

Knowing the enemy's intentions helps us with that pesky problem of expectations that we keep facing in the parental universe. We deal with disappointments and pressure over incorrect expectations for ourselves, but we also deal with being blindsided and not preparing ourselves to expect what our enemy is actively trying to do to destroy our families. We need not be afraid, but we need not be idle either.

Above all, our expectations for what God wants to do in our families will dictate so much of the ways we not only survive but thrive in parenting. The apostle Paul wrote, "Therefore, there is now no condemnation for those who are in Christ Jesus" (Romans 8:1). If you face your day expecting God's constant critique of your parenting skills, then your expectations of his nature are skewed in the wrong direction. Do you trust him with your successes and your failures? Then he has not one ounce of condemnation for you—and when you expect that kind of attitude from him toward you as you face the mayhem of any given day, it changes the way you feel and respond.

Trusting Christ and rightly believing that he sees you through his grace takes that old ugly backpack from your shoulders because you realize it's not yours to carry. But just because you do this, don't stop expecting your enemy to keep doing what your enemy does. Satan will keep trying all day long to get us to hyperfocus on our mistakes and inadequacies. It's actually the oldest trick in the book. He may be pretty persuasive, but Satan is really not that creative. If you know what to expect, you don't have to be surprised by his daily attacks.

The day of the infamous wall-kicking debacle, I kept giving in and listening to Satan's lies. He tried to distract me. Instead of focusing on what was actually happening, I focused on the fact that Dave was not home. That was the real root of my frustration, yet I wasn't dealing with it; I was burying it. I needed to bring it to God in prayer. Shame and anger always make us look down, but Christ always lifts up our heads.

Looking back now at my thirty-four-year-old self, I would say to her, "Yes, kicking a hole in the wall was a mistake. You let your anger turn into sin for sure. But oh, young and unwrinkled Ann, lift up your head! This whole parenting thing doesn't hinge on you doing everything right or not doing anything wrong. You got grace, kid! In fact, you actually did some things right too." Let's look at those, because Satan will never remind you of the good.

1. You were present with your kids today.
2. You prayed before you got out of bed that God would help you be a good wife and mom.
3. You fed your kids and fed yourself (yes, let's count the little things).
4. You got yourself and everyone dressed (woo-hoo!).
5. You put on makeup (bonus points here). This was for Dave's benefit and to not scare the children.
6. You packed lunches (fairly healthy to boot).
7. You drove your kids to school and prayed out loud with them about the day (discipleship).
8. You got a ton of work done and played with Cody.
9. You made dinner and played fun music as the boys played.
10. You helped with homework. (Yes, this is where the bad part snuck in, but don't stop there.)
11. You apologized to your kids and asked for their forgiveness (teaching conflict resolution skills).
12. You prayed and asked forgiveness from God out loud, in front of the kids, and asked him to help you display self-control as a fruit of the Spirit (discipleship).
13. You kissed them good night, laid your hand on them, and prayed for them.
14. You cleaned up the house before going to bed.
15. You read your Bible (okay, only a few verses because you couldn't concentrate, but still).

16. You had sex with Dave. (Honestly, you can't remember, but if you did, that's a win too! But you probably didn't because you were still wallowing in guilt.)

Wow! Looking back, my thirty-four-year-old self should have been awarded a gold star or a trophy . . . or a Blizzard from Dairy Queen (what the heck, make it bigger than the junior size). I hadn't been perfect, but God wasn't requiring perfection. His grace was covering the missed targets, freeing me to aim again without shame.

The truth is, my heavenly Father was probably already saying all these things to me, but I was too busy listening to the enemy's lies to hear the applause of unconditional love, as well as his still small voice. He still whispers to each of us an invitation, which is especially nourishing to those of us who carry a backpack full of guilt while we raise small children. He says, "Come to me, all you who are weary and burdened, and I will give you rest. Take my yoke [that means 'backpack' in Greek] upon you and learn from me, for I am gentle and humble in heart, and you will find *rest* for your souls. For my yoke [backpack] is easy and my burden is light" (Matthew 11:28–30, emphasis mine).

Mom or Dad, the discipline and training stages for your kids begin with you disciplining and training yourself to keep taking off that nasty, stinky backpack of guilt and shame. It's not helping you. In fact, it's hindering you from the freedom that comes from running the race of life alongside Jesus. And you can't raise kids who won't carry this backpack themselves if all you ever do is carry it in front of them.

So just give it to Jesus. He'll know what to do with it. And with you.

— Reflections —

FIRST SON: CJ

- It was never obvious when we were kids that Mom was feeling guilt about her parenting at all.
- I have much more vivid memories of her being fun and happy than her ever being sad or frustrated.
- There was a difference between when she was mad at us for being bad and when she was mad from just being frustrated. During the times she was frustrated, like when she kicked the hole in the wall, it didn't feel like she was taking it out on us. That just seems like a crazy story we could tell Dad and our friends. She was always back to normal and fun the next day.
- Mom's letters, which she would often write after waking up at 2:00 a.m., usually felt unneeded to me. She'd always just reiterate things that were obvious from interacting with her every day. She was just saying what I already knew.

CHAPTER 6

YOUR LOVELY LITTLE *Sinner-lings*

When I (Dave) think back to those first twelve years of our children's lives, many distinctive memories and impressions flood my mind. The first one is that I had hair—well, if a really embarrassing comb-over counts, then I had a little hair. I also remember the exhaustion. This is not a dramatic or funny thing—I mean it was a true sense of feeling exhausted all the time because we just didn't sleep very much. Maybe you can relate. When it comes to sleep during these early years, the struggle is very real.

When we teach at our parenting conferences, Ann often describes a vivid memory that occurred when our boys were five years old, three years old, and five months old, respectively. (Yes, she could tell this story herself, but I think it would honor her more if I told it because I will say things about her that she would never say about herself . . . true things.) At the time, I was traveling with the Lions for a road game, and Ann was getting the boys ready for bed. It happened to be the first time she was able to sit down all day while she nursed our youngest, Cody. She was beyond exhausted.

She had just sat down while the two older boys were in the bathtub. Just then, the doorbell rang. This interrupted Cody's feeding time, and since he was starving, just like any Wilson male is at any given moment, he began screaming in protest. Just then, she heard our oldest son CJ yelling, "Mommy, Mommy, I have to go poopy right now!"

She yelled back, "Honey, you're in the bathroom already, so just get out of the tub and go!"

"No. I don't want Austin to see me!" That may be foolproof logic to a five-year-old, but it makes my head hurt just thinking about it—and I wasn't even the one this was happening to. CJ was intent on preserving his poopy privacy, so he got out of the tub and began running down the hall, completely soaked and naked.

The doorbell rang again.

Ann was trying to get to the door when she heard, "Oh, no! I went poopy on the carpet!" Austin heard CJ's declaration and just had to see for himself, ergo a second naked and wet little boy was now running through the house. Austin began laughing at CJ for the "mess" he had made, which started a fight between them. CJ was screaming at the top of his lungs as he chased Austin around the house. Austin was also screaming. Cody had never stopped screaming. And what the heck, the dog, cat, and fish began screaming as well—and we didn't even have a fish or a cat, if that tells you anything.

Ann finally reached the door, opening it only to discover it was a magazine salesman. Needless to say, that guy didn't make a sale at our house that day. Regardless, the "butterfly effect" of parenting during the toddler years is a fascinating and terrifying reality . . . one errant doorbell can unleash an unholy sequence of events that engulfs the house in poop, screams, and absolute pandemonium.

The truth is, I didn't always get exactly how hard this stage was. I understand it now, but I didn't always understand it then. During experiences like this weekend debacle, I would come home from another Lions road loss, collapse in the chair, and say, "I'm totally exhausted!" I meant it, but I just didn't get it.

I had flown on a chartered flight, ate wonderfully catered meals, and slept in a fabulous hotel room all to myself—right before riding with a police escort to the stadium and to the airport. Oh yeah, and I also watched an NFL football game from the sideline. Boy, it was a really tough life I was living. Yet when I got home, I actually thought my weekend was harder than Ann's. I couldn't have been more wrong.

Over time, I learned from Ann because I began listening to her struggles—and those conversations weren't always easy. Even so, there's no use avoiding them because raising toddlers is hard work that never seems to end. Perhaps this is why dads often sit on the toilet for hours just to get a break from it. Okay, maybe not hours, but certainly longer than necessary.

If you're honest, you know I'm right.

Our time and sleep aren't the only things affected during this stage. Once when Ann and I were speaking together at an event, she asked me what I remember most about parenting during the toddler years. Without really thinking, I heard myself say, "I remember not having sex very much." Not my finest hour, but I was just being honest. Truthfully, kids are omnipresent in your space during this stage, hanging off you, following you to the bathroom, and needing your constant attention, even when you just want to eat dinner like a human for five minutes. (They need you to scoop the food off their faces and redeposit it into their mouths. It's cute, but it doesn't exactly beg for candlelight.)

It felt like Ann didn't really want me to touch her that often because she was being touched by little kids every single minute of every single day. The last thing she wanted was another person trying to touch her—and besides, we both knew if I touched her too much, we could end up having another kid, and then the whole cycle would only get crazier.

Of course I'm just kidding . . . mostly.

These impressions and memories during this season of kids only prove that parenting is a wonderful and sometimes terrifying ride filled with ups and downs—and that anyone who is on this ride has moments when he or she does not know what's coming next or how to respond to it. The good news is that the Bible is rich in parenting wisdom, principles, truths, and commands, most of which people seem to not know. In fact, there is an especially large cache of biblical wisdom regarding how to navigate the first twelve years of your children's lives.

These principles helped us identify our bull's-eye and also offered us insights on how to hit that target with an actual strategy. This strategy for engaging in the first two stages—discipline and training—begins by discovering what is most important during these formative years.

I love the New Testament book of Ephesians because it is so practical. The apostle Paul wrote a six-chapter letter to a church he had planted in Ephesus. The first three chapters are about theology and doctrine, while the final three chapters are practical applications of this theology. Paul *first* shares what is true about the identity of God and ourselves. And *then,* based on the foundation of these solid doctrines, he writes about how we should live as a result of these truths.

In chapter 5, Paul applies helpful truths to our marriages and our relationships, culminating in chapter 6, where he applies these truths to our families—and specifically to our parenting. Keep in mind that Paul's version of this book was not a book with chapters, but just a letter to friends he was discipling. This flow from marriage and relationships into family and parenting wasn't a separate topic, but rather a natural flow of thought they would have recognized.

In Ephesians 6:1–3, Paul writes, "Children, obey your parents in the Lord, for this is right. 'Honor your father and mother'—which is the first commandment with a promise—'so that it may go well with you and that you may enjoy long life on the earth.'"

As parents, we tend to love this verse because it directly commands our kids to honor and obey us. It's like our biblical ace in the hole—our trump card for any situation. We love these kinds of things in the Bible because they appear to be direct and simple. However, Paul feels the need to not only show us *what* should happen but also describe *how* it should happen.

Honor is the result of obedience. This is why there are two things being described in this verse: obedience and an attitude of honor found in that obedience. One can technically obey their parents without honoring them—that would be an action of the hands. However, obeying and honoring one's parents is an action of the heart. To honor your father and mother requires an attitude of respect. The right kind of honor is actually developed in our kids as we give them the right kind of training that relates to what obedience should really look like.

Again, keep in mind the stage we're in here, namely, the *early stages*. This is not about dictatorship or dominance; it's about the right kind of boundaries found in the right kind of disciplines that lead to the right kind of training that can help them eventually have the right kind of attitudes as adults.

So when children are very young, parents should establish the boundaries—some may call them "the rules"—of the house. These won't hurt your kids; in fact, they'll do the opposite. Kids at these tender ages don't have a concept for how to obey appropriately, which is a key to developing maturity in their attitudes and viewpoints down the road. This is why we call this the discipline stage—and it's not meant to last forever.

Parents need to *establish* the rules of the home and then *enforce* these rules when they are challenged. And yes, they will be challenged, probably daily. This is natural for little ones who have never experienced the concept of boundaries before. They must explore them, and you must help them know which ones are flexible and which ones are rigid. This is how they learn.

From the beginning, this stage is super important because we are not training them to just obey us, but also to obey God. This is not to say we should shame them by throwing the "God card" in their faces when they disobey. They are going to disobey, just as we are. Why? Because they are human, which makes them broken. Yes, they are sinners—and this does not diminish their value before God or before you. As broken people, they are not less precious to their Father or to their earthly parents. But my point is that they are not going to obey you at first—expect this. There is no reason to shame or stigmatize them for it by calling them "bad kids" or kids who are "disappointing Jesus." Instead, just expect them to be kids who are learning discipline through your tutelage.

Besides, if they are sinners (or little "sinner-lings" as we used to call it), where do you really think they learned the sinful behavior of humanity? News flash: they got it from us, their sinner parents!

The first five years are crucial in this obedience training because it can stick with them for their whole lives. We will make mistakes, but we must keep recommitting to doing it well. This doesn't mean it is easy; in fact, it may be the hardest thing you ever do as a young parent. Also, it can seem to be never-ending because they keep pushing the boundaries over and over again. But don't give up—remember that the payoff for your discipline now will come years down the road.

A rule is like a fence. As a parent, we need to first establish that boundary—or build the fence. This means clearly defining the rule. Maybe we say, "You can't go into the street on your Big Wheel, and if you do, you'll go to bed at seven o'clock." This rule, like all of them you will create, is established because we love them and want to protect them. This is the same reason God gives us his Word—his boundaries for living. I used to look at the Bible as a set of rules to keep me from having fun, but now I can see that God sets boundaries because he loves us and wants to protect us, leading us to the life we feel instinctively wired to pursue. In fact, this concept is actually a lot easier to accept when you have little ones of your own because you know that you do the same for your kids, even if they don't understand or like it.

What do we do when God sets a boundary for us? Instinctively, we try to breach it. We try to go beyond it. So guess what your child is going to do once you establish a boundary? They are going to inch their way—or ride their Big Wheels full speed—toward that boundary to see if it will be enforced. Every child will do this at some point, even those who don't seem to push your buttons as much. We should not be surprised when they challenge our rules; rather, we should expect it. This doesn't mean your kid is a bad kid. It means he or she is a normal kid—a *sinner-ling* loved by God and being redeemed by the same gospel process that is redeeming you as well.

USING YOUR HEAD WITHOUT LOSING YOUR MIND

Once when Ann and I were teaching about this concept from the stage, I brought out one of those child gates we put in our homes to keep children out of certain areas. I wanted to illustrate that children are going to bang up against their parents' fence—that is, whatever rule you've just laid down. So I got down on my knees and banged my head against the child gate to show that every kid will push the limits.

Well, I guess I banged my head a little too hard on the gate because it cut the skin right off my bald head. Blood began flowing everywhere! To this day, I imagine that our church remembered that particular illustration pretty well.

The truth is, if we don't discipline well during this stage, we will be the ones who keep hitting our heads against the sharp edges of experiences down the road. This is why we must keep our heads about us during this stage, which includes not being surprised when our toddlers push up against our rules.

The topic of Big Wheels comes up a lot at this age. When CJ was two years old, we got him his own Big Wheels so he could scurry around on our driveway. On the first day we gave it to him, we established the boundary. We took him to the end of our driveway and said, "CJ, you cannot go past this line at the end of the driveway. If you go past this line, you could get hurt, and we'll take the Big Wheel away from you for a time."

He looked at us with those sweet, innocent eyes and compliantly replied, "Okay." What a great kid! A perfect specimen of sweetness and maturity beyond his years. A picture of innocence and . . . *wait, he's heading for the street!*

It took all of five minutes before he went down to the end of the driveway and stopped. He looked right back at Ann and me—and then he did it. It was intentional. It was premeditated (for five minutes, but that's a long time for a two-year-old). It was ruthless. And yet he took that front wheel and slid it right out into the street. He even had a smirk on his face as he did it, boldly challenging the almighty dad of the universe.

So what's a parent to do? We must enforce the boundary. We ran down there and made sure he knew that the rule would be upheld by Mom and Dad. Very little emotion is needed for moments like these—again, be careful not to associate their behavior with their identity. Avoid saying things like, "You are a disobedient kid!" That messaging can get stuck in there somewhere down deep. It may sound like semantics, but it's always a better choice to separate behavior from the character you want them to have. "You are acting like a disobedient kid, and I know that's not who you are!" In this case, they are told who they really are, not that their behavior has defined their identity.

The harsh truth you must expect is that these kinds of moments of disobedience will happen multiple times a day—or sometimes multiple times an hour, depending on the number of kids you have. As parents, we so easily just become weary and give up on the disciplining—no one wants to feel like the Gestapo in their own home (hopefully). Beware not to give in to the exhaustion during this stage by moving the boundary just a little to acquiesce and create a little peace for yourself. If you start moving the boundary little bits at a time, there's a chance you will look up and no longer have any boundaries at all.

This is worth repeating and reinforcing, so hear me again. Once you set the boundary and they bump up against it, enforce the boundary immediately. If you move the boundary, they win—and in this case, it means they lose down the road because they won't have the foundations for obedience that lead to so many other important things in life and faith. So if you maintain the boundary, they will actually be learning what obedience looks like.

Yes, they will scream and yell and kick and call you all kinds of names, especially as they get older, but don't let what's happening on the outside cause you to miss what's happening on the inside. I know it's hard and you think you can't do it, but you *can* do it—and you *have* to do it, especially in the early years. The crazy thing is that when you do it, they feel safe. No, they will never tell you that—their crying fits and tantrums can make you think you're doing the wrong thing. You aren't, unless your boundary is cruel or unreasonable, or being used as a weapon against them—don't taunt them with it or use it as a way to rule as a tyrant. Just let it be what it is.

Fences protect us and make us feel secure and safe; they will cause your children to feel safe as well. Especially when they become adults and have to obey rules they don't like in the moment, they will have been taught that those rules bring safety and protection to their lives. So use your head here, and don't lose your mind.

A seemingly counterintuitive effect of enforced boundaries is freedom. It doesn't sound logical, but it's true. Once kids feel safe inside the fence, the yard becomes their ultimate playland. They will climb the trees, run recklessly in the green grass, and dance in the sprinkler as if you have taken them to a water park—and they will know that everything within the boundaries you have established is theirs, a good gift from their parent to explore.

Boundaries are liberating, not confining. Choosing their own boundaries in the big and dangerous world outside that fence may seem alluring to them, but it is too big with too many choices that are beyond their ability to make. Life outside the fence would stress them out at that age—and also hurt them.

They may *cry* for life outside the fence, but they will *laugh* fully and freely—as children should be able to do—within the boundaries.

Again, the trick is consistency. Don't *give up*, and eventually they'll realize you love them enough to not *give in*. Believe it or not, over time, you will start to see kids who are doing what you say, when you say it, with a good attitude. Not perfectly, but at times it will truly occur. Without boundaries, it will seldom occur. For the Wilsons, it didn't always work perfectly. At times, it was a war. But we had to be willing to fight the right kinds of battles so our home wouldn't become a child-centered home. Boundaries keep a home from becoming a place where the child is in control. If you let them, they will become the parent and you will become the kid who is constantly trying to keep up with their demands and ever-changing whims. It is unhealthy and unsustainable for both of you, but it can happen.

DISCIPLINE OVER TIME

Ann here—I just have to chime in on these final points about the discipline stage. As I recently led a small group of women, a young mom began complaining that her four-year-old daughter bites everyone in sight. "She bites me! She bites her dad! She bites her sister! I can't even take her to playgroup because she bites everybody."

I felt her pain. Children can be very strong-willed, stubborn, and pigheaded, especially when they develop or fixate on a certain pattern or behavior. I knew she was embarrassed and was hurting over the issue. After I listened and shared in her pain for a few minutes, I felt invited by her to gently engage again. "If you don't mind me asking, what are you going to do about it?"

She sighed in exasperated surrender. "I guess I'm going to take her to preschool and hope that the preschool teacher can get her biting under control."

This was hard because she felt she had no other option, but I had to love her well enough to call her back to the consistency of boundary making that this stage requires.

"Girlfriend, teachers can help, and we all need outside assistance from community, but just remember that this is not the school's or the church's job; this is *your* job."

I know why she was losing heart. It was the constant repetition of it all. Who among us can keep saying and doing the same things over and over again without seeing any results in return? It's hard, but think of these years as a timed challenge. For the first five years, no matter what your children say or do in return, enforce boundaries over and over again. Just set your mind that you're going to do it, come hell or high water, until five years have passed.

We've been around parents who say they never get to talk to each other in the evening because their kids won't go to bed. Now we all know how hard it can be to train a baby or toddler to sleep on their own, but it must be done or your marriage will suffer. Recently, one of our sons (you can guess which one) was struggling to get his one-year-old to sleep through the night. No matter what, the baby just wouldn't sleep on his own. Our son told his wife, "I've got this. I'm going in there to just rub his back a bit until he goes to sleep. I'll be back in a few." Minutes passed. Then hours. Finally, when his wife looked at the baby monitor to see what was going on, she saw her husband all curled up in the crib (not kidding—a grown man in a crib!), fast asleep with their son! That's one way to do it.

Obviously, it's a ton of work—there's no two ways about it. So as parents, we must keep doing the hardest work early on to make sure our home is adult-run and not a case of "the baby running the crib," so to speak.

One of the keys to teaching obedience and honor is to ensure there are consequences for our children's actions. Every choice we make in life has consequences. Good choices yield good consequences, and bad choices yield bad consequences. Sure, life isn't always this simple in the gray areas of adulthood, but for children, a healthy understanding of the basic principles of consequences are like the nails that hold the fence together.

As you set boundaries, be sure the consequences—good and bad—are spelled out clearly beforehand so they know what will happen if they decide to choose the bad option. Don't do what I (Dave) often did. When one of the boys didn't do what I told him when I told him, I would start yelling to get him to take action. For quite some time, I didn't realize I was training my boys to disobey me until I began yelling. In their minds, the thought was, *Dad doesn't really mean business until he starts yelling.* When we scream, we actually teach our kids to disregard what we say until it is followed by this emotional outburst.

Another ineffective phrase parents often use is, "I'm going to count to three." This really means the child can disregard everything the parent has said until he or she gets to two and a half. Yes, it can be a tactic to give them time to choose the right thing, but when this tactic must be used every time, it creates a learned behavior to never do what has been said the moment it has been said.

Looking back, I can now see that many times, my kids didn't obey until I yelled and then counted to a magic number—and we disciplined them into these patterns, though not on purpose. Thank God for grandkids. I feel like I have a much better handle on this children thing the second time around.

Again, in this discipline and obedience stage, the consequences we choose are important. They may involve a loss of privileges or a time-out. We used both of these in spades in our home—and every once in a rare moment, we would spank. We tailored the consequences to each child because each child was so very different. For one of our sons, a time-out was all it took for him to immediately want to obey. This wasn't the case for the other two.

To be clear, we never spanked for anything but outright disobedience. We know this is a sensitive issue, as it should be. We do not condone intense physical punishment at any age. So, when we use the term *spank*, we're not talking about whaling on a kid. Spanking can become abuse, so it must be used only in certain situations and only when it can be dispensed outside of a state of anger. Never spank if you're in a state of anger. Use another tool in your toolbox or take some time to cool off first.

I (Ann) rarely ever spanked, even when Dave wasn't home. However, at times an appropriate spanking was warranted. This usually happened after one of the boys would choose to flagrantly disobey a rule. I would say, "Go into the other room and wait for me," and they would sit there in a chair, like a time-out, and wait for me to come into the room. I never wanted to discipline in anger, so I had to take some time to myself. I would be so angry at times that I would need for them to be removed from my sight for a minute or two so I could gather myself. There were times when I would say, "Get to the other room now! Run!"

Their response usually indicated I had gotten their attention. Their initial response as they marched with head down to the waiting room was the emotional equivalent of, *Oh no! Mom's really mad!*

Discipline of any kind, including appropriate spanking, should always be an act of love used as a tool to teach children something valuable to their own well-being. If we're honest with ourselves, we know when we're in an active state of anger that may cause us to overdo any kind of discipline, including verbal correction, versus when we're in a place where we may still be perturbed over the behavior but are in complete control of our emotions. It may take time to move from the first emotional place to the second, but waiting until you get there is super important.

When I would finally make it into the waiting room of ill repute (the waiting was sometimes just as effective as the discipline itself), I'd sit down across from them and say, "What did you do wrong? Why was I upset? What boundary did you cross?" It was important that they had a clear understanding of what they had done wrong. I had a little wooden spoon and would quickly spank them—only on their bottoms—and then we would talk about it. And then we would pray together.

It wasn't a long process, but having any kind of process helped me to not just swat at them every time I got mad. If we spank out of anger, very little learning is going on. Did we do it perfectly? Not even close. Parenting is a moving target, even when we know our bull's-eye. But we did learn that the more consistent we were as parents, the better results we saw with our boys.

We also found that when we asked them to do something or stated a rule, it was important to make sure we really had their attention. They could easily drift off and not be attentive, so we learned to touch them on the shoulder or hands as we explained something to them. This touch would help them connect with our words. We'd then ask them to repeat back what we had said so we could make sure they had heard and understood.

Ann sometimes does this with me (Dave)—not because I'm a child (I have the birth certificate and hairline to prove otherwise), but because the technique works well for anyone. The phone is a major factor in whether or not we hear one another—men, women, or children alike (though children at this age shouldn't have phones). Sometimes Ann will take my phone out of my hand, look me in the eye, and ask, "What did I just say?" I'm embarrassed to admit that half the time, I have no idea what she just said. Your kids are probably no different.

Finally, try to avoid creating an overly heavy environment of discipline, even if your kids are constantly misbehaving. There is a balance here, but if you're always dropping the hammer, even appropriately, it can become exhausting for everyone involved. It can also diminish the effectiveness of your approach, making you wonder if any of it is sticking. If you yell all the time, yelling just becomes normal for your kids—and now you'll have to escalate past the *normal* yelling if you want to *really* get their attention.

You don't want to create a culture in your home in which no one, even yourself, would really want to live. You can be consistent without keeping your home in a state of DEFCON 2, locking everything down as if there is a breach to the nuclear core. The nuclear core you are guarding should be more nuclear *family* and less nuclear *missile*. You are raising a family, not an army.

Stay consistent, but don't miss the fun of it all. Children are a gift from God that brings joy to your lives, often through the very chaos they create that you are trying to manage. Your efforts will pay off in the long run. Trust us again—you can't evaluate the effectiveness of your efforts *during* these first five years, just as you can't evaluate how strong and sturdy an oak tree will be while its seed is still hidden in the unseen places beneath the soil. You'll have to trust the vertical here—the One who sees beneath the soil. Keep watering. Keep weeding. Keep waiting. God knows what he's doing, even when you're not so sure about yourself.

In fact, you can rest assured that you will blow it as parents during this stage—and probably often. A vertical parenting perspective reminds us that we're not the ones who ultimately decide the outcomes of our children, even though we have a crucial role. Our mistakes don't have to tank our kids. Grace abounds, so we should humbly seek grace at every turn. When you say or do something you regret, go to your children and apologize. If you expect them to be consistent, you must be consistent in this area too. When you know you are wrong but refuse to admit it, you're teaching them that the principles of your family are just for children—and they will have good reason to discard them the moment they are not under your hypocritical, authoritarian rule.

This may sound harsh, but we've met many teens and young adults who feel this way about their parents and their "rules." If humility and repentance are what you say matter for your kids, the only way to make sure these goals aren't just words is to lead by example in being humble and repentant. If you're worried about losing your superior position of authority, don't be. If locking down your home leads you to lock down your own heart, it's only a matter of time before it all blows up anyway. It would be better for you to blow it up with humility now—shock your children with your own authentic confession of wrong attitudes, words, and actions. Tell them how you blew it, and ask for their forgiveness. You're not giving them power you'll never regain; you're giving them invaluable lessons about what strong adults really do in real life.

By the way, you will usually discover what Jesus meant when he said we must come to him like little children. Little children have an easier "God connection" than adults. This is why you will be shockingly encouraged by how quickly and easily your kids will offer you the very grace and forgiveness that God offers us all but that we adults sometimes struggle to receive. It is a beautiful, divine experience to be loved and forgiven by your own children—like a valuable diamond that is gift wrapped in preschool wrapping paper. I remember driving home with our three little boys in the car when I said, "Guys, I'm sorry I got so mad in the store. I shouldn't have yelled at you like that. I was wrong." CJ, who was seven at the time, immediately chirped, "That's okay, Dad. We're all idiots sometimes."

Truer words have never been spoken.

If you are reading this and you realize you haven't done your job to discipline your kids, don't despair. God's grace is still present and able to make a difference. No matter what your children's ages are (unless they're adults—then the conversation is a bit different), start by going to them and saying, "I'm sorry. I've neglected my responsibility to discipline and train you. I need to step up and help you become the person God is making you into. So here we go. Here are the rules from this point forward." Yes, they may not like it, but you must begin to trust in the long-term outcomes.

It's never too late. Start today. It'll be a war, so hang in there. You have the weapons to fight *for* your kids and not against them. Cling to your faith. Cling to your spouse. If you don't have a spouse, then cling to a trusted community that will help you keep clinging to God.

— Reflections —

SECOND SON: AUSTIN

I have four kids—five years old and younger—so this chapter applies directly to our current stage of parenting. Here are some reflections from a dad in the midst of this sleep-deprived, diaper-filled instructional stage.

- Pray with your kids throughout the day—not just before meals and before bed. Pray on the way to school and in moments of discipline.
- If you fight with your spouse in front of your kids, be sure to forgive each other in front of your kids as well.
- Dads, get in there and change diapers! Be up in the middle of the night when your kids are sick, teething, or just awake in those early months. Your wife's job of instructing and parenting your kids is more important than your day job, so share in the sleep deprivation.
- Play with your kids. Make-believe with them, be silly, wrestle, and throw them in the air (just make sure you catch them or they have a soft place to land). My parents did this really well, and I have fond memories from this stage of life.
- Get down on your child's level physically. This applies to play, as well as to discipline and instruction. Eye contact and connection are so important in this stage.
- Touch, hug, and kiss your kids as many times as possible throughout the day.

CHAPTER 7

THE *Minivan Days*

Training Stage, Ages Five to Twelve

When your kids are very young and you are in the disciplining stage, you feel like you're scurrying about endlessly from one task, need, problem, or lesson to the next. It is overstimulating at times. In the beginning, they can't eat without you, walk without you, take a bath without you, or even poop without you—and they sure do poop a lot!

Even though they do begin walking and talking after a short time, this doesn't suddenly remove their constant need for you to be present at every step. After all, now you have to block the stairs so they don't fall, manage the bites of food so they don't choke, and try to control their outbursts in the store, at church, or while you're on a work call—and that can get real complicated when all work calls are Zoom calls from home. Thank God for the video and mute buttons!

This season feels like it will never end, but it does. Then you will enter a stage unlike any other—the training stage when they are between the ages of five and twelve. Some of the fondest memories of raising children will occur during this stage. In theory, they can now eat on their own, walk on their own without randomly falling down the stairs, take baths on their own (though you may have to start the water and stay close enough to engage if there are rubber ducky emergencies), and, yes, mostly poop on their own. Well, sort of.

The best and most important part of the training stage is the fact that you can begin to have actual conversations with your children. It is no longer just the beautiful babbling of baby talk or the never-ending reinforcement of rules. They will begin paying attention to street signs, TV commercials, your conversations with your spouse (often much to your chagrin), and everything else imaginable. It's as if they are suddenly aware of the outside world and are curious and fascinated by everything they see and experience.

And if you play your cards right, you have the honor of being the filter through which all of this curiosity flows, which means you will have as much or more influence during this stage than any other. Now this does not mean your conversations with them will always be deep and meaningful, though they often will be. This is a season of exposure and setting expectations.

It will be hard at times as your kids begin to discover that the world outside the fences you have built for them is not nearly as safe. They will begin asking questions about what they see in the world or overhear before you can find the mute button on the news channel you're watching. "Why are those people so mad?" You will sigh, but this is the training stage, and you have the opportunity to break down in digestible amounts the truths about war, racism, oppression, crime, and the like. Again, it hurts, because everything inside you wants to keep them safely within your fence where none of those things can reach them. However, they are officially training for their own journey outside the fence, so you have to help them understand what they see.

Much of this stage is not heavy, but rather fun and joyful! They will be your little buddies who pile into the restaurant booth next to you for pancakes and say the darndest things—sometimes silly and sometimes surprisingly profound. Soak it in. Engage them with the influence you have while you have it; in a few years, the influence will still be there, but they will be in a different stage of receiving it. Take pictures. Journal about your trips and conversations. Hug them tight and kiss their precious faces.

And above all, take the training stage seriously—this is when your influence matters the most.

If we look back at Paul's instructions in the sixth chapter of Ephesians, we find an important instruction for parents that applies to the training stage. "Fathers, do not exasperate your children; instead, bring them up in the training and instruction of the Lord" (Ephesians 6:4). Paul directs this command to fathers, but it applies to both fathers and mothers.

How do we exasperate our children? In light of the context of what Paul has just written, we can exasperate our kids when we don't discipline and train them appropriately, such as when we inconsistently enforce boundaries or when we react instead of listening, repenting, and engaging them. Most training that is effective doesn't just happen spontaneously; it is intentional, even if it is applied to spontaneous situations that arise.

Instead of exasperating our children—leaving them to train themselves in ways they don't know how to do, we are invited by God to train and instruct them in the ways of the Lord. Nothing is more tragic than stories of children who had no one to discipline and train them in love—who had to survive in difficult situations where there was no parent or guardian present or where the parent or guardian present was neglectful or even abusive.

Children should not have to find their own way. Scripture *leads us* to *lead them* with love and patience. Don't miss the direct implication of this verse. God does not want children to be exasperated—that is, constantly frustrated or maddened—by their childhood experiences. Yes, this may also feel like a moving target because so much of training and discipline is difficult and involves pointing out things that need to be corrected or done differently. But this is what this stage entails, so even though there is a constant state of correction, it doesn't have to mean there is a constant state of exasperation. The goal is to keep helping your kids accept the process of training as a positive part of their lives, even when you constantly point out areas that need adjustment; these teachable moments don't have to be thought of as negative.

In athletics, training is a constant process that precedes the actual game. Depending on the sport, games may happen between once and three times a week during the season. Training, on the other hand, happens constantly every single day. Athletes would never dare to wait until the game to begin training—at that point, the goal is that all the training from every other day has become second nature. The athlete should now just repeat on the field or court what they've done a million other times when the lights and cameras were not turned on.

In this way, training involves isolating little things so they can be worked on without the pressure of everything else the game requires. Layup drills are safe. You can do them for hours—and it doesn't really matter if you miss a bunch of them. That's the point. And though when the game finally comes, it won't require only layups, those drills in the training stage will ensure that the skill is present and easily accessible when the situation calls for it.

Parenting in this stage is exactly the same concept: helping your children repeat smaller components of what they will need for real-life situations in safe, doable, safe-to-fail spurts. No harm or foul if they miss the target here—it's not yet the "game" of teen years and adulthood when they will need to put it all together in real-life situations.

Scripture is saying that your job as a parent is to lead your kids to the truths and practices—especially the spiritual ones—they will need to survive and thrive in the future. Again, this is *not* the church's job or the Christian school's job. We must accept that it is the parents' job.

A TALL (BUT FUN) ORDER

It may surprise you to hear, but for me (Dave), the toughest part of being a dad was leading my home spiritually. I know it sounds crazy, what with me being a full-time pastor and chaplain. I think many of us who are dads share the same feelings, along with plenty of moms as well.

The truth is, I found it so much easier to preach to and lead thousands of people at my church who were *not* my offspring than to lead Ann and my three boys in our home. It would be easier to let people assume otherwise, but it simply wasn't the case.

I can remember coming home after any given Sunday and looking forward to crashing because I was so exhausted. My Sunday routine entailed preaching three morning services at church before racing down to Ford Field to work on the Lions sideline during the game. After the game, I would often counsel players and coaches in the locker room, and it wasn't uncommon for me to not make it home until 7:00 p.m.

After a late dinner and watching a little Sunday Night

Football (because I obviously needed more football), I'd head up to bed with Ann around 10:00 p.m. On one night in particular, I was just beginning to doze off into blissful sleep when Ann said, "I sure wish that the guy who leads our church so strongly actually lived in this house with us." I was barely conscious, but I definitely caught her drift.

"What did you just say?"

"I just wish you would bring the same energy to spiritually leading me and our family that you bring to leading our church."

It was a dagger—and like most daggers, it cut deep. To this day, I still can't fully recall exactly what came out of my mouth, but her words had lit a fuse in me. I propped myself up in bed and yelled something to the effect of, "Woman [always a good start], you don't know how good you have it. I am the best husband and dad I know. You should be the most grateful woman on the planet!"

I probably wasn't foolish enough to actually say it exactly like that. Probably. After spewing whatever it was that came out of my mouth, I rolled over and went to sleep. Or at least I tried to.

This was not one of those things that just evaporated away with the next morning's sunrise. Ann's words rang in my ears, and as mad as they made me, I had the feeling I needed to hear them. That's when I sat with God and went vertical. I asked him if he was speaking to me through Ann—I almost immediately sensed the answer was yes.

As I sat in a quiet moment alone with Jesus, I came to the same conclusion that Ann had dropped on me like a bomb the night before: I was bringing more energy and passion to my job as a pastor than I was to my job as a husband and father. My life and attitude could have been a case study for misplaced priorities. Ironically, I was the guy who preached to all the other men that our wives and kids are more important than our jobs—and yet I wasn't practicing what I preached. Ann's words to me that night were a wake-up call from God to step up and begin leading my family spiritually to a degree that surpassed my leadership at church. I didn't just need to work harder at home; my leadership efforts needed to reflect that my home was more important than church—because it was.

Maybe this could be a wake-up call for you as well.

When I really dug deeper into the problem, I realized it was easier to feel confident in my ability to lead my church than my family. I went to seminary and have attended many seminars and conferences on how to be a better leader in my role as a pastor. I feel equipped in that role, and I mostly know what to do. But when I came home and saw my wife and kids looking to me to lead them spiritually, I froze up. There was no college or seminary that ever taught me what to do when your kids need you to play with them but you feel drained of energy, or when they freak out for the seventy-fifth time that day and you don't know how to address it without losing your mind. My tendency was to become passive. It became all too easy to just expect Ann to get it done.

And she does "get it done," but she has always rightly longed for me to lead her and the kids by serving them as well as—well, actually by serving them better than—everyone else I serve in ministry and in life. As a dad of three grown sons and a grandfather of five, I have regrets about my passivity in this area. We'll all make mistakes and have things to regret as parents, but trust me, you don't want to have regrets related to a lack of effort. If I could go back and do it over, I would simply engage more. I would get out of the chair and come alongside my wife to lead and love these kids spiritually. This is my charge to you.

You are going to blink, and they will be gone. Step up today and create a "no regrets" parenting plan.

And by the way, this isn't just a dad issue. Many parents struggle in homes where one of them engages more intentionally while the other hangs back in passivity, content to just let the other lead. Obviously, if you are a single parent, you have no choice—and God will fully equip you to lead as you must. He will give you what you need, which will include a godly community to share in your parenting.

But for those homes with both parents, how can we spiritually lead our home as equal partners? I find a great answer in a classic Scripture that was a key for the nation of Israel in regard to passing on their faith to the next generation. This text is so foundational that an Israelite recited it several times a day as one of the pillars of their faith, as well as the foundation for their family. It instructs us on how to pass on spiritual truths to our children. And you'll probably recognize some of these words, because Jesus quoted this passage when he was asked which of the commandments was the most important.

> Hear, O Israel: The LORD our God, the LORD is one. Love the LORD your God with all your heart and with all your soul and with all your strength. These commandments that I give you today are to be on your hearts. Impress them on your children. Talk about them when you sit at home and when you walk along the road, when you lie down and when you get up.
>
> *Deuteronomy 6:4–7*

This passage is where the first *L* of our bull's-eye for our kids comes from: *love God*. Yes, parenting is a tall order. There are so many things, especially during the training stage, that will require our constant attention. However, if we can lay our heads on our pillows at night and say that we loved God with all we had that day, then we can call it a good day. This is also the hope for our kids—a clear vertical target that can help everyone in the family. Putting this first will free you and your children to keep the most important thing at the forefront rather than just hoping it happens.

How do we lead them and pass along this most important thing every day? We find the answer in the passage. We are to impress onto our children the beauty of the Holy Spirit who resides and is being cultivated in us. To be clear, this isn't about making your kids just recite Scripture or listen to you talk about Jesus for hours on end; this is about an authentic overflow of what is happening in the parent's soul. If your home feels like a mess and you can't keep up, welcome to the club. However, just remember that the chaos may not be what you need to be talking about and correcting the most.

As a parent, are you resting in the grace of Christ today? Are you confident that he is on your side, working out his greater purposes in your good and bad circumstances? Are you aligning your life and bringing your brokenness into the light of his gospel? Are you refusing to isolate from his people but instead pursuing authentic relationships where you can confess *the real you* so others can love, pray for, counsel, and sharpen you like iron?

While none of us are perfect in these areas, if these are not at least a part of your intentions and pursuits today, then let's talk about *that* before we talk about all the things you need to fix with your kids. This growth in discipleship isn't something that occurs by just doing more spiritual disciplines. Don't take the questions above and add them to an endless checklist of things not being accomplished in your life. To do so will only lead to shame and frustration, which is the opposite of resting in the grace of God. This is a heart thing. Even if you don't have a lot of time, you can truly assess where your heart is in today's chaos and begin dealing with it, using a simple prayer: "Jesus, I am overwhelmed, behind, and frustrated, but I choose to put you first. Please let my relationship with you affect my life right here, right now."

Don't ever forget this truth: You cannot lead your children to a place you've never been. We can't give away what we don't first possess ourselves.

If Jesus is the most important relationship in our lives, then God's love will overflow from him to us to our kids. We will naturally talk about Jesus at the dinner table. We will naturally talk about him when we take walks or go on trips. We will naturally talk about him when we're putting our kids to bed and when we wake up. It won't be highfalutin Jesus talk; it will be real Jesus talk. Not fabricated, but rather genuine and sincere—an overflow of what is in our souls.

- "You know, honey, Mommy struggles with that same issue all the time. I'm learning to ask Jesus to help me every time it comes up. Do you want to ask him together to do the same for you?"
- "My day went great! I was in an important meeting and things weren't going well, but then I know that Jesus gave me a great idea!"
- "I know you're angry—that's okay. Just remember that God's Word reminds us to be angry, but don't sin. How can we process what you're feeling without missing our family target?"

When these kinds of conversations become second nature, we invite God to transform our first natures—our sinful natures.

I have studied and taught this passage for decades and I've never been more convinced that we as parents are called by God to train and instruct our children in the ways of the Lord. It's just that too often we don't know what those ways really are. Direct your energy to learning his ways for yourself, and loving God will become a natural overflow of refreshment for your kids rather than a made-up fire hose of religious jargon and shame.

Parents are often encouraged to establish college funds for their kids as an intentional investment in their future. Since we know they won't be little kids forever, it seems irresponsible to avoid planning for the next stage in the best way we can. Starting a college fund means depositing an initial amount of money and then adding to it consistently over time—which is a really good idea, by the way.

Developing a love for God and his ways among your family is like establishing a spiritual college fund for your kids. You don't have to have it all at once, meaning you may struggle yourself in many spiritual areas. That's okay—college funds aren't built overnight. They take years of consistent contributions, some big and some small. In the same way, begin making consistent contributions to your kids' concepts of God, grace, the gospel, community, and the like. Even when they are infants, begin to deposit spiritual truth into them daily so they'll have a treasure trove by the time the training stage ends. In this case, their spiritual college fund will also pay dividends when they do end up going to college. It's a win-win.

The point here is to seize the moments during these years to "bring them up in the training and instruction of the Lord" (Ephesians 6:4). They are curious and hungry to learn, so take hold of their curiosity and make it fun. They really want to know who God is, but perhaps you feel inadequate to help because you yourself struggle with faith or are new to the faith.

Maybe when you open the Bible, it just appears to be the longest book you've ever seen with no rhyme or reason—you wouldn't even know where to begin.

Let me encourage you to remember that the overflow you will pass along to your kids is not an overflow of perfection or knowledge; it is an overflow of trust in God that leads you to grow in front of them and with them. You don't need to be a scholar to help your family learn and grow closer to Christ—especially if you always focus on the humble process of growing yourself.

Church is crucial here. The church is literally God's idea for this very thing—the making of disciples of all ages. For many people, when they hear this, they immediately think we're talking about taking your kids to church so someone else can teach them something we don't know ourselves. While this may happen at times, this isn't at all what I mean.

Being a part of God's family in true community is the only context in which you can grow yourself, which is necessary if you're going to help your kids grow in the faith as well. It is not a series of classes, a gauntlet of activities to keep everyone busy, or a really good children or youth pastor who is going to make all of this click for you or your kids. What will make it click is God's people living according to God's ways together, and doing so in the light of real community.

And yes, within these relationships, you will read books, watch videos, listen to sermons, have discussions, and the like. Just remember that while it's always good to access the abundance of resources like devotionals, kids Bibles, and family studies available online and in Christian bookstores these days, they are most effective when everyone is using them to learn how to grow in right relationships with other believers. As you train your children, this will let you and your kids actually experience what you are training for in the field of play, so to speak.

Loving and serving others in real relationships—complete with commitments, conflict, and care—will make the training make so much more sense. Jesus will do in them what all of your best intentions as a teacher or resource provider could never do in a hundred years. It takes the pressure to transform hearts off of you and puts it where it belongs—on Jesus.

Some time ago, Ann was leading a Bible study with some of the young moms who were wives of the Detroit Lions players. She was emphasizing that it's our job as parents to train our kids to live and follow God's ways. One of the moms spoke up and said, "Tell me what to do because I don't know anything."

Ann replied, "You can start by picking up a kids Bible and just start reading it with your kids. But make it fun. Don't say, 'Okay, children, now is our time to read God's Word, so you better sit still and pay attention.' It needs to be fun because God's Word is life-giving and full of wisdom and adventure, so we should have an attitude about it that is also life-giving and adventurous."

This young mom took Ann's advice to heart and simply began reading from a kids Bible at night with her kids. When she reported back to Ann, she was amazed at the incredible stories she had never read before. It affected her kids, but it affected her deeply as well, so much so that after her kids fell asleep, she'd often take the kids Bible into her bedroom and keep reading because it was so good.

That is the essence of overflow. You don't have to be perfect in knowledge or application of truth before you try to influence your kids. Think of it this way: gravity is a fundamental truth, right? It was true before you were born; it was true before you believed it; it will continue to be true even if you struggle with it; and it will remain true long after your time on this earth is over. In other words, truth doesn't hinge on you. It is secure with or without your knowledge or mastery of it.

The same is true of God's grace. You don't have to be an expert for it to still work or for you to share it with your kids, even while you're still learning and being affected by it yourself. In fact, the most effective method for their effective engagement with the gospel can be watching a real person they trust more than anyone else wrestle and grow in honesty. Even so, it is definitely wise to not go it alone. Yes, start on your own, but add to your own journey the influence of those who may be further down the road than you and whose knowledge of Scripture and discipleship is wider than yours. This is especially effective with another mom or dad with whom you can discover these truths together.

And no matter what, don't be afraid to *not* have all the answers with your kids. You can do unintentional damage to their spiritual understanding and viewpoints by speculating beyond your understanding of God's Word. If you don't know the answers to your kids' questions, it's okay to say, "That's a great question. I'm really not sure, so let's go find the answer together." If you do this, you'll be training them not just to be knowledgeable but also to be humble and teachable, and to not feel isolated in their present or future spiritual journeys. You don't have to be *telling* them something in order to be training them. You are training them in everything you *do* and in everything you *don't* do.

EMBRACING THE FUN AND THE OPPORTUNITY OF TRAINING

In our kids' early years, Ann was extraordinarily good at making training fun for the family. As she'll discuss in greater detail, part of this comes from her unique personality and the way she is wired for fun and excitement. I understand this is not everyone's natural or default disposition in life, which is just fine. You don't have to be a trickster, jokester, or prankster at heart to bring a little fun to the training. Any parent can find the fun if they keep in mind the reality that kids are kids.

When it comes to the things of God, our joy, excitement, and, yes, our sense of fun will be transferred to them. If we're not careful, we can involuntarily cause them to be about as excited about God as taxes, insurance, or colonoscopies. If our demeanor toward spiritual things is essentially the same as it is toward all of these areas, why should our kids' demeanors not follow suit?

This is not about watering it down—not in the least. Yes, it has to be on their level, but that doesn't mean it has to be shallow. Engage in conversations about God's ways in the middle of conflicts and miscommunications. After all, you'll have a lot of opportunity for these kinds of conversations. When you pray, use real words they can understand and thank God not just for the regular "prayer" type things (the food, good sleep, world peace, and the like), but also for fun things or even funny things. Let your kids find that prayer is a place where real conversations occur that include both tears and laughter alike. Trust me, they will not always be sitting down or sitting still during these prayer times. Let them move around. Challenge yourself to be okay with that.

Several things Ann did while training our kids stick out in my memory. Once she organized a Bible scavenger hunt by hiding little pieces of paper with verses around the yard. Whoever found the final verse got a dollar bill. The kids ate it up—and not just for the dollar, though that didn't hurt.

Another time, Ann and the boys were on their way to church when she pulled into a restaurant parking lot. "I thought we were going to church," the boys said.

"You know what?" Ann replied. "Sometimes it can feel like a certain thing is the only plan in your life, but life can change suddenly because God begins taking you in another direction. You've got to be ready for God to take you to great and unexpected places, so we're going to eat a great breakfast together. But remember, sometimes God will take you down a path that is really hard—and you won't want to go there because you hate it. But God is there too, and he grows us in those hard times." The boys listened because she found a way to take a daily experience and make it creative and fun while also preparing them for difficult moments in their future. Also, they got to skip church that day—and it was perfectly fine.

Now I get to watch Ann do the same thing with our grandkids. The good news, however, is that you don't have to be a master to engage your kids. Just do something, and do it with gusto.

For what it's worth, when CJ was in his twenties, I asked him if he remembered the breakfast trip and the great truths his mom taught them. "No, I don't remember all the truths," he replied honestly, "but I do remember eating breakfast that morning. It was awesome!"

They may not remember the details or even all the lessons, but they will remember the way your caring, sincere heart made them feel. That'll stick with them for a lifetime. It will give them a foundation. The thing is, God himself is the One who will build on those foundations of love, honesty, and creativity later in their lives.

There are so many ways to pass on these spiritual truths. One is to sit down with the whole family and study the Bible together. Ann always wanted me to do this with our boys, but truthfully, it wasn't really my style. I was much more of a "as you walk along the way" kind of dad. I loved to identify teachable moments in everyday life and try to apply God's truth to those experiences.

I'll never forget walking through a mall with all three of my boys when they were eleven, nine, and six years old. CJ hit puberty early and was beginning to become interested in girls. As we walked through the mall, I noticed a magazine rack located low to the ground in the center of the mall hallway. Positioned directly on the front of this magazine rack was a bikini magazine with a girl on the cover who was barely covered by any fabric. I was walking behind the boys, so I had a bird's-eye view of whether they'd notice the magazine. Austin and Cody were oblivious to the entire magazine rack, but CJ definitely took a glance at the girl on the cover. It was hard to miss since she was right at eye level.

It was a normal moment all boys face, and I knew it would happen countless other times in his future. Normal moments are the best time to train. We can't expect children to suddenly gain knowledge, wisdom, and strength to deal with more difficult temptations if we don't make the most of "normal" moments.

As soon as we passed the magazines, I stopped CJ for a quick second and asked, "Did you see that magazine rack back there?" He said, "No!" Yep, kids can become super embarrassed in this stage, especially when you have conversations of value with them. Don't sweat this—lean into it with honesty and authenticity, the things you want to be formed in them.

"I saw it," I said. He looked up at me curiously.

"Yeah, I saw it too."

I became even more specific. "Did you see the girl in the bikini on the front of the magazine?"

"No, I didn't see that."

"Well, I saw her." Again, he looked at me and followed my lead.

"Yeah, I saw her too."

"Did you want to look at her?" We were past the shallows now.

"No, not really."

"I did. I wanted to look."

This time, he sheepishly looked at me. "Me too."

Is this a moment of spiritual training? More than you'll ever know. Confession. Honesty. Not avoiding obvious issues. Trust. Vulnerability. It was all surfacing right there in the mall. My dad never had this kind of "dad talk" with me about sexual temptation and purity. But I get to write a new legacy with my family—and so do you.

I took a knee next to him and said, "CJ, it's normal to want to look at that girl. She's beautiful, and God has made us to appreciate beauty. Your desire to look is not a bad thing, but we men have to be careful. She didn't have much clothing on, and I never want to look at another woman like that other than your mom, especially when they're in a bathing suit."

He may have been embarrassed, but the topic had his attention.

"So you know what I do? When I see something I want to look at so bad but know doesn't honor God or your mom, I try to turn my eyes away from it. I protect my eyes and keep them only for your mom. Son, this stuff will be difficult for you as you grow up, but it's super important for you to protect your eyes. Trust me, where we look as men will lead us to what we do as men. So let's make a pact to protect our eyes together."

"Okay, Dad."

And that was it. It took all of five minutes. I wasn't even sure CJ remembered, so I recently asked him about it. He said it taught him that it wasn't embarrassing to say he saw the girl in the swimsuit because wanting to look at girls was normal, but he needed to be very careful with his eyes. It was a chance to seize an opportunity to pour into my son an important set of truths about a struggle that will be with him, with me, and with every man for our entire lives. It wasn't about just that one moment; it was about those kinds of moments being normal and happening regularly in our lives.

It was just another day of training.

CHAPTER 8

MAKE YOUR HOME THE *Haven They Run To*

Thirty years ago, we helped start a new church with two other remarkable families. We were vacationing with one of them once—Paula and Steve and their family—when we all needed to pile into their minivan to go somewhere to eat. Once the doors were closed, I (Ann) noticed that there was something unique playing through their car speakers.

It was some great classic work of literature—and I don't even remember which one it was, which lets you know how much I know about great classics of literature.

I was impressed. Paula and Steve must have been more well-read than I realized.

"Do you and Paula enjoy this book?" I asked innocently.

"Oh, no," Steve assured us. "It's actually our kids who love listening to it."

Heart. Drop.

"It's just soooo good, isn't it?" It was less of a question and more of an uppity pronouncement of fact. Now mind you, none of our kids—or their kids—were over the age of ten, as far as I recall. I happened to glance over at one of our kids to find that his finger was shoved so far up his nose that it had to be touching the bottom of his nonclassically trained brain, or what was left of it. I think he was searching the recesses of his nose for a predinner snack. Their kid was listening to the classics, while my kid was looking for the "classic" go-to grub of infants and animals.

Head. Drop.

Ever been there? I sure have. I used to compare myself and my kids to *everyone* around me. Comparison had a stranglehold on me stronger than my youngest's death grip on whatever foreign and toxic object he had just yanked out of his little nose. The curse of comparison felt especially severe during the discipline and training years—and we didn't even have social media back then.

This is not a male or female issue; it's a human issue. Some of us may love to proclaim that we really don't care what people think of us, and perhaps a few of us can really mean it. However, most people do care—and some who go far out of their way to proclaim they don't are just trying to create a smoke screen to mask how they really feel. As the classical literature families might say, "They doth protest too much, methinks."

Regardless of how severely this may affect you, I think we can agree that comparison sucks the life and energy out of us. It paralyzes us, keeping us from seeing the greatness in our own kids because we're so busy wishing our kids, our family, or our marriages were more like the classical literature folks (or connoisseurs, as they call themselves—a term no real human can spell without spell-check).

Seriously though, when comparison takes hold, our kids never win. For that matter, neither do we. We know this, but much like the knowledge that we shouldn't eat a half gallon of ice cream at 10:00 p.m., many of us still find ourselves wiping traces of chocolate sin from our lips the next morning. (I'm not mentioning any names here, but it rhymes with brave.)

You can't just snap your fingers and make the temptation to compare yourself to others go away. It is around us everywhere. Every time we see a television show with someone else's family, read a post about someone else's kid's accomplishments at school, have a conversation at work about someone else's kid's progress on the soccer team, or sit in a moms group and hear about someone else's kid's ability to take that first step, pass that next milestone, or say the cutest thing, we can't help but compare it to our own experiences. And even if our kids happen to excel in a variety of areas, we can still be tempted to evaluate their progress in direct comparison to others. "Whew, my kid seems to be doing better than the ________ kid, so I guess we're okay."

It's not just about comparing kids either. Every comparison about *them* leads us to instinctively compare ourselves to *their* parents. A cycle of shame or overconfidence in the wrong things keeps many parents swirling about in either insecurity or unfounded judgment of other parents. But there are many variables in play beyond just our parenting. It's easy to forget we can't control the outcomes of our kids' lives.

Kids come prewired with unique personalities, dispositions, strengths, and, yes, weaknesses. Some are athletic, while others excel in academics. Some can see a flower and draw it with precision at the age of ten, while others struggle to color between the lines. Some are strong in social situations, while others become shy and withdrawn in groups. The point is that there is more to the equation than just our parenting. We must learn to refuse to internalize all the credit or all the blame for their positive and negative traits.

As parents, we are *managers* and *stewards* of this process, not creators. *The* Creator is the only One truly big enough to handle the creating.

Overcoming comparison issues often requires a revolution in the heart, so let's explore ways to help our hearts get out of this trap.

HAVEN THINKING FOR HEART CHANGE

Have you ever thought to yourself, *This world is so big and so dark and they'll face so many challenges, so what do I know? What if I don't get everything right that they need to learn?* The training stage reveals our perceived deficiencies. We want to impart everything our kids will need in order to grow into healthy adults, but we can't.

For me, a conversation with my close friend Callie really opened my eyes to a comforting yet truely vertical perspective. One day, she casually said she knew God had picked her to be the parent of her children, who were both biological and adopted. She knew he had chosen her and no one else, so God must know she had exactly what her kids needed.

This sounds a little self-aggrandizing until you get to the core of what she was saying. She was not saying she had no faults, understood everything her kids needed, and was the answer to all of their problems. Not in the least. Instead, she was taking refuge in the truth of God's sovereignty and his promise to direct our steps, if we invite him to do so. This means he was the one with no fault, full understanding, and, more importantly, was the answer to all of their problems. This goes back to the manager versus creator idea. God is the owner, but he grants us stewardship of various parts of his creation, including his kids, whom we get to call "our kids" as well. But as people, they are under his creative purview, not ours.

The parable of the bags of gold gives us a perfect glimpse into this concept and reveals ways we are more ready for the tasks of parenting than we might think. Matthew 25:14–15 reads:

> "Again, it will be like a man going on a journey, who called his servants and entrusted his wealth to them. To one he gave five bags of gold, to another two bags, and to another one bag, *each according to his ability.* Then he went on his journey" (emphasis mine).

Did you catch it? The master entrusted what was valuable to him to servants who were also valuable to him, and he only gave them what he knew they could handle—that is, *according to their ability.* This can be such an insulting concept in a comparison world because we all tend to approach every issue with the unspoken feeling that we are all equal in ability. Yes, we are equal in worth, but we are not equal in ability. This shouldn't be an insult; it should be a comfort.

Callie had grasped this concept. God had given her exactly what she could be successful at stewarding as a parent—and at the end of this parable, everything goes back to the master anyway. God lets us share in the raising of his kids, but we don't have a higher level of love, concern, or affection for them. I don't think this means we ever have to completely give them back. I think God intends for us to enjoy our loved ones together for eternity. I do, however, think it means we have to remember whose they are and who we've given them over to—that is, we must release ourselves from the errant notion that their complete growth, future, and outcomes are solely dependent on us. That's a lot of unnecessary pressure, and it simply isn't true.

When Callie introduced this concept to me, I couldn't get it out of my head. Once again, however, comparison and insecurity are not just issues of the head, but more so of the heart.

I understood what she was saying, and I found myself longing to have that level of confidence and security in my heart. It took some time, but the information eventually began to produce transformation.

I began to believe that God designed *me* knowing the kids I would have under my roof. He had already equipped me with passions, talents, ideas, and a personality that our kids needed. I didn't have to feel out of place in my own home or even in my own skin. He was the Master who had the ultimate control over their outcome, and I had been tasked with helping to manage the ones he loved so dearly—a task for which I was uniquely suited because he had lined up my life's situations with my abilities to handle them.

This changed everything. Instead of hating myself or constantly trying to change everything about myself to become worthy of this impossible task, I began to explore who God had already made me to be. When the condemnation of comparison wasn't my primary concern, I was free to ask questions like, *Who am I?* and *What is important to me?* This was a perfect fit with the bull's-eye concepts we were already exploring. I began praying more than just for God to change me to be a better parent. That's a fine prayer we should all pray at times, but it can lead us into assuming that God didn't already know what he was doing when he placed these kids with us. I added to this prayer a request for God to help me know what he had uniquely placed within me that I could easily give to our kids.

As I began to seek this path, a Josh McDowell quote resurfaced in my head: "Rules without relationships lead to rebellions."[1] This felt so right. I didn't desire a house of only rules—I

1. Quoted in Sean McDowell, "Three Important Lessons about Parenting," Sean McDowell (blog), August 6, 2015, https://seanmcdowell.org/blog/three-important-lessons-about-parenting.

desired a great relationship with each of my kids. I wanted our relationship to be a haven for them, even when they were struggling or breaking the rules.

I also thought about my parents and my upbringing. You've heard Dave's tragic childhood story; mine was so different. Life with my parents, my sister, and my two brothers was a wonderful haven where I felt safe and cared for. In fact, as a kid, I wanted to be at home more than anywhere else because it felt better than any party I could have gone to.

Isn't it funny how my story and Dave's story can both lead to unhealthy comparisons? That's the way comparisons work. They are always unhealthy, no matter how healthy some of the things being compared may seem to be. For Dave, he needed to use his experiences as motivation to pivot the environment and experiences for his kids into a completely different direction. For me, I needed to stop comparing myself to my amazing parents and instead learn from them and become more comfortable with leaning into my own experiences as a parent, complete with all of their imperfections.

I looked at all I had learned from my parents and all I was trying to unlearn from negative experiences. I considered what was unique to me and eventually came up with some simple takeaways. The first came out of a simple question: *What do I want in my home?*

- Jesus is *everything.*
- Joy and laughter should permeate our home.

I began with only these two things because I didn't want to put any additional undue expectations on myself, only to fail. "Jesus is everything" was a goal we had already established with our family mission. It just needed to be incorporated into the culture we were really fostering at home, not the one we thought we should foster compared to others.

The second goal of infusing joy and laughter into every part of our lives accented the first goal of making Jesus everything. Following Jesus was going to bring joy, not rob us of it. Thus for both of the targets, "Let's make a memory" became a suitable mantra. It also fit well with my personality. I began to find ways to fit what mattered with the way I was designed.

Making memories has always made sense to me. I guess you could say it's one of the ways I combat the negativity in the world. When I'm down, it's great to have something in my mind to turn to—a memory of moments when I was "up," which can remind me of safe places in life and that the positive moments will happen yet again, if I don't give up.

Life is hard at times. It hurts to watch our kids experience life's difficulties, but it can't be avoided. Kids at school can be mean. The world has its daily share of catastrophes with COVID-19, death, sexual abuse, wars raging around the world, racial discrimination and violence right here in our own backyards, and destruction of life on a grand scale. Our kids are feeling the weight of these issues, which is why suicide rates are on the rise, and depression and anxiety are advancing to record levels.

I get it. It makes me sad to even have to address these things, especially in the context of our kids. I wish they didn't have to face any of it. I wish they could be free from the worry of it all. But the reality is, I'm training them to face a broken world.

So how does this fit into your unique calling as their parent? Ask the question, *What if my home could become a haven in the midst of these storms?*

We tend to think we are protecting our kids from the stress of it all. In fact, we get frustrated when they become stressed, because, after all, they don't even really understand the half of what's really going on in this crazy world. They don't know everything we're shielding them from.

Even so, life *is* stressful, and they are feeling it too. You can alleviate it to some degree, but you cannot remove it. Beyond that, you can't parent away the brokenness within them. That's Jesus' job. He will use the difficulties of the world as one of his tools to grow them in grace and trust, just as he did for you. You can't remove the risk and the realities. They are feeling it right now, whether you realize it or not.

The truth is that kids today feel less safe than any generation before them. Consider what they have to think about, which most of us could never have imagined when we were growing up. Active shooters entering their schools. Terrorist attacks. Global pandemics. Online bullying. And a host of other problems because they are the first generation of kids who, because of phones and social media, are bombarded with news twenty-four hours a day, just as we adults are.

As they become more and more exposed to these devastating realities, they need to know where they can feel safe when nothing in this world guarantees safety.

That's where you come in.

BEING THE UNIQUELY CREATED YOU

Your home will be an extension of you. The air of your house will carry your unique personality. In order for your home to be a haven for your family, you must know who you are. So who are you? What are your motivations and strengths? Through what lenses do you tend to view the world?

If you don't know, it's time to begin exploring. Don't assume you completely understand what's inside your own noggin. Knowing ourselves is one of the most complex tasks in our lives. It is easy to boil it down to our behaviors, but they can't fully describe who you really are. Instead of thinking only about what you do, try to discover *why* you do what you do.

For example, two people may both insist on keeping a clean house. It would be easy to assume they're doing it for the same reasons, but this is usually not the case. One person may want a clean house out of a desire to bring something in their chaotic life under control. This is a tangible, accomplishable way to tell their crazy life what to do rather than the other way around. Another person may want a clean house because in their mind, a clean house is the way a house is supposed to be—one of those black-and-white issues of life that has no gray area. If you really want to break it down, a third person may want a clean house out of a desire to prove to those who live there how much they love them by keeping the space tidy and accessible to their needs.

Three people doing the same things out of completely different motivations—do not underestimate how important these unique motivations are to the goal of discovering why you do what you do.

Discovering how you're made is a long journey. It may help to begin by asking your kids, spouse, friends, and family a few specific questions about yourself. *What do you think matters to me the most? When I'm under stress, how do you think I respond to the situation? What do you think makes me happy? When you have a problem, do you approach me differently than someone else? If so, how?*

Tools are available to help you learn more about yourself. Then you can invite Jesus into deeper parts of your heart, mind, and strength. Tools like the ones I'm about to discuss will pick the locks to some rooms you may not have even known existed beforehand. You may not like these kinds of things, but I can truthfully say that some of them have helped remind me and inform me of who God has made me to be.

One tool is the Enneagram. The word *Enneagram* comes from two Greek words—*ennea*, which means "nine," and *gramma*, which means "written" or "drawn." It is not actually a test, even though there are many tests out there. Many Enneagram practitioners recommend reading a book or attending a seminar rather than just taking a test. The idea is that you shouldn't want to immediately identify and self-describe under one of the nine numbers. Again, the path to learning more about the way you are uniquely made isn't created overnight—and it shouldn't end at a simple destination. There may be nine numbers in this ancient study of interconnected typology, but no one is just one thing; there are infinite possibilities, and you are one of those "one in a million."

Don't worry, the Enneagram hasn't replaced my Bible. It has led me to invite Scripture into the deeper parts of my psyche, parts I now understand better. I'm a Seven, which is "The Enthusiast."[2] If you know anything about the Enneagram, you know that Sevens tend to like to have fun and be on an adventure constantly. We like new things and sometimes pursue risky things. We also tend to have a hidden agenda: avoiding pain at any cost.

Hmm, now how could this help me know myself as a parent?

On the CliftonStrengths assessment, my first strength is "Activator."[3] This made so much sense to me. I would become

2. For more detail, see "The Enthusiast: Enneagram Type Seven," Enneagram Institute, www.enneagraminstitute.com/type-7.

3. For more detail, see "An Introduction to the Activator CliftonStrengths Theme," Gallup, www.gallup.com/cliftonstrengths/en/252140/activator-theme.aspx.

bored if I ever had to sit around the house all day long. Notice I said "*if* I ever had to." That tells you how often I just sit around. I also become easily bored when I have to do the same thing every day. Positivity is also in my top five strengths. Joy comes fairly easy to me, which makes sense because I usually see the glass as half full.

The Myers-Briggs Type Indicator is another tool I've used to help me understand myself better. I am an ESTP.[4] I know, you need a decoder ring for all of these. Unsurprisingly, this just means I would generally be described as outgoing, action-oriented, and dramatic. Again, no type on any personality assessment tool will completely describe anyone to a tee, but these resonate with me, as I am a planner in certain areas, yet I don't like to be pinned down by excessive planning that limits fun and spontaneity. I may be more likely than others to improvise and keep my options open.

Looking back, I can see how various personality types were evident in my own parents, though I didn't understand it on this level back then. My dad seemed to have a lot of these same characteristics, which would explain why every winter, we kept a trampoline in our low-ceiling basement . . . you know, just for fun. My dad also takes great delight in telling me I was conceived on the trampoline, information fun for him to communicate but not so fun for me to hear.

Dad also set up stations in our basement that included a basketball hoop, a ball on a string that we could hit with a baseball bat, and a rocking horse he made by hand out of a wine barrel on springs—complete with a real saddle on top. We spent so many incredibly fun days in that little unfinished basement, persevering through the cold months of winter in

4. For more detail, see "MBTI Basics," Myers and Briggs Foundation, www.myersbriggs.org/my-mbti-personality-type/mbti-basics.

Ohio. It was most definitely a haven, not because of the stuff, but because of my parents.

When our kids began to reach the training stage, Dave and I began to plan how we could create a haven, not only for our kids, but for all the neighbor kids as well. We wanted our home to be the place where every kid on the block wanted to come. Now keep in mind that our finances were similar to missionaries. We had to raise financial support for Dave to be the chaplain for the Detroit Lions, plus we were in the early years of church planting. We weren't exactly raking in piles of money.

So we pinched pennies and saved every spare dollar until we could afford a trampoline. We had a friend who was building a new deck and wanted to get rid of the lumber from the old one. Dave took it off his hands and repurposed the old wood into a *Swiss Family Robinson*–style tree house . . . well, kind of. It did lack the running water systems, makeshift elevators, and multiple buildings in multiple trees. Otherwise though, it was identical.

We also transformed our unfinished basement into a fun house for the kids. Honestly, it was embarrassing for our friends with beautifully finished basements to see it. I shook that off because I was done with the comparison idol. I was embracing who God made me to be as a person and as a parent. Our basement wonderland was equipped with a slide, a Little Tikes swing hanging from the rafters, a regular swing, a trapeze (with a twin-size mattress beneath it), a full-size punching bag, and a hanging rope to climb or to use to swing over to the beat-up couch we had bought and "installed" as the launching and landing pad for swinging.

I told you it was embarrassing—and I loved every minute of it, once I got over myself.

We also included a reading corner because I wanted our

kids to love reading. The room was filled with stuffed animals for the younger boys, a box of costumes for transforming into their favorite heroes, and a workbench where any of them, but especially CJ, would spend hours tearing mechanical things apart and attempting to reassemble them.

It was just stuff, but it was so much more than that; it was their haven in our home. The place where they could fully embrace being kids. Did it protect them from the dangers and issues of the broken world that were coming for them? No. Yet it was our hope that it would give them the feeling of love, safety, and fun that kids should feel with their parents, both earthly and heavenly. It was a memory maker, and those memories became intricately interwoven into the big picture of their lives and future in ways we would never be able to fully identify. We just wanted this haven to become a part of them—something to build on.

Should you do something similar in your house, bonus room, or basement? Again, this is about knowing yourself, so do it only if it fits who you are and who your kids are.

As grandparents, we've had so much fun watching our kids with their own kids, especially when they create their own spaces for their kids to thrive, grow, and laugh. Every time we leave Austin and Kendall's house, we are blown away at the home they have created for their young family. Neighborhood kids are running in and out of the house. They are welcoming to every straggler on the street. Dave and I were giddy to hang up a few swings and ropes in their basement to continue the legacy of laughter and, yes, sometimes tears, as fighting ensued over the toys.

Cody and Jenna have also begun their own version with their young family, though their kids aren't yet in the training stage. But even for littles, there are ways to create these magical adventures that establish your home as a haven—ways that are unique to your own unique personality as their God-given parent.

When our kids were moving between stages, I realized we were spending a lot of time in the car, which meant there was opportunity I had been missing. I have a pretty vivid imagination, so I attempted to make the vehicle another place of adventure for them. We'd pretend the car was a jet. I'd tell them to get ready for takeoff and buckle their seat belts—which helped me to get them to buckle their seat belts. Added bonus.

I'd rev the minivan engine and they would think we were about to go a hundred miles an hour. I would floor it and send us skyrocketing forward in our speeding jet—speeding at about thirty miles per hour. To them, it was a real jet, and they were my real copilots. Sometimes we'd drive around in circles over and over again on the dead-end street by our house. Our neighbors probably thought I was insane, but oh the laughter in that car! Honestly, it still brings tears to my eyes as I recall the absolute squeals of joy in our little jet.

"Do it again! Do it again!"

The adults may have thought I was crazy (and they may have been right), but every kid in the neighborhood looked on with jealous eyes. They would have given anything to be in that car with us! Do you know why? Joy and laughter are contagious. Everyone wants to be around them.

We took hikes into the woods with lunches packed and books in our backpacks. We found walking sticks perfect for hiking. The other girls and boys in the neighborhood were our coconspirators as we hunted snakes and toads, picked flowers, and read books on our newly discovered tract of land we coined our own "Lost Boys Island." We were into *Peter Pan* in those days, but being in the story was even better than just reading it.

I could go on and on about camping in our woods, tree houses, spraying the trampoline with shaving cream and sliding around on it, Slip 'N Slides with whipped cream, blow-up pools filled with warm water, and bicycle ramps.

Dave was no slacker in this department either. It never failed that if the Michigan afternoon weather was decent enough, I'd find him outside after a long day of work playing every game imaginable with the boys. Roller hockey, freeze tag, kickball, capture the flag, football, baseball, basketball—you name it. Our boys enjoyed those games because Dave made them fun. It became the neighborhood joke that all the older boys in the neighborhood would ring our doorbell asking if Mr. Wilson could come out to play.

You see, joy is a magnet, and everyone in the neighborhood was drawn to it. Kids want to be around adults who are fun. We can't always be fun, but that doesn't mean we should *never* be fun. These adventures comprise some of my favorite memories as a mom. Not every parent can or will play outside with their kids, and that's okay. It worked for us, and I think that when it can work for you, it's a good idea to try. Over time, we developed good relationships with all the neighborhood families, so they came to trust us, which made life fuller for our boys because they had so many extra playmates.

Keep in mind that this was an extension of me discovering my own unique wiring. It would have been easy to think we needed to keep the boys inside all the time, studying Scripture and literature and whatnot. We could have done that, and it might have still been good for them, but it wasn't a good fit with who we were as parents.

I know I've described a lot of wacky hijinks and fun, and perhaps that's just not you. That's okay. It doesn't mean you can't find ways to have fun with your kids in a way that spurs memories within them of the haven your home was for them. Take them out to special dinners. Plan special trips. Sit and talk through your days creatively. Try asking them at the dinner table: What was one good thing that happened to you today, one bad thing, and one nice thing you did for someone else today?

It is about knowing yourself and using your unique expressions to create special memories for your own family—and this will often bleed over into others' lives as well. Many times over those years, we would eat dinner or lunch with those same kids in the neighborhood. We'd always pray and often share stories from the Bible, revealing the gospel to them in a way that helped them understand Jesus' love for them. This was a great experience for our kids to witness. We didn't have to take them door-to-door to share the gospel with strangers. The kids came through our doors instead. Later in the evening, our family would pray that our kids' sweet little neighborhood friends would say yes to the invitation of a Savior who loved them so dearly. Our home wasn't just a haven for our own kids; it also became a magnet for other kids. In this respect, we were beginning to hit our bull's-eye of "making a dent where we are sent."

THORNS AND EYES AND SUCH

I again remind you of where we began with this chapter—avoiding comparison. So before you start thinking I'm a pied piper of children, let me be the first to assure you that my heart wasn't always in it. Many times, Dave and I did these things when all we really wanted to do was sit in the house and watch a relaxing show to soothe our frayed nerves. We often made ourselves go outside because we wanted to build a haven for our kids, but sometimes we were just too tired.

We didn't always get it right, but we aimed at a target that worked for us. Even if we missed it, we knew what to aim at the next day. This is the power of knowing how you are made. You can position your family's target within the boundaries of your unique outlook and life. That way, when it doesn't go according to plan, you don't have to throw up your hands in despair or punish yourself with endless comparisons to others. You know your own target well, and you realize the goal is not to hit it just one time. Rather, your goal is for the principles and attitudes of your target to become memorable and second nature to your kids. This won't be decided on one good or one bad day.

And there will be bad days. It's okay. Grace gives you a reset button, so push it.

I remember one summer night in particular when things didn't go according to plan. I was finishing up dishes in the kitchen, watching a dozen kids play in the backyard through the window over the sink. Dave was out of town, and I was utterly exhausted—you know, *that* kind of tired, the kind that finds you counting down the minutes until bedtime comes and you can finally take a break for the first time since your kids' beautiful but intruding voices awakened you at 6:30 a.m. I glanced at the clock. Only a few more hours, and I could take a shower and maybe sit, read, and rest like a human before sleep overtook me.

Suddenly, ten-year-old CJ threw open the door and interrupted my fantasies about bathing and reading a book for five minutes (you know, parent fantasies). He was completely out of breath from running.

"Mom, we need you!" he shrieked.

His urgency alarmed me, and I wondered what had happened—and if it would ruin my possible rest with another trip to the emergency room for the latest set of stitches.

"Why? What happened?" I asked, putting down the dish towel, ready to spring into action, as vigilant EMT moms sometimes have to do. My noble readiness to meet any crisis head-on seemed to irritate him. You know how kids can be so wrapped up in their own worlds that they don't realize how dramatic they've made an everyday moment? This was one of those times. It's no wonder our hair begins turning gray (or begins letting loose, as it were) during these years.

"No, Mom! We need one more person for capture the flag. The teams aren't even, and we need you to play!"

"Ohhhh," I said in a tone of relief, which again irritated CJ. This was serious business to him. "Honey, I've got some things to finish. You guys will be fine without me," I picked up the dish towel and once again began to dream my way toward my respite, which was still a real possibility.

Disappointment etched his face as he slowly walked out of the kitchen, knowing he would be the bearer of bad news to the thirteen-year-old friends he really wanted to impress. Guilt or the Holy Spirit (sometimes it's hard to distinguish one from the other, but the more I learn how I'm made, the easier it's becoming) began to tug at my mindstrings. (You've heard of heartstrings, so why not?)

How much longer is he going to be running into the house begging me to play a game with him?

I took a breath. This was going to put me behind on dishes and other housework, which meant I could kiss my evening book time goodbye. But as Dave said earlier, you blink, and they're gone, so I put the dish towel down, grabbed my little Keds slip-ons, and walked out to the backyard. As I emerged into view, a collective cheer went up from the kids.

"Okay, I'm ready to play. What are the teams?" I looked over at my boys, and they were grinning from ear to ear.

Hold on to this moment, I told myself. *They still think you're super cool.* Consequently, they also still thought I was super fast—poor, ignorant children whom I loved so much.

After teams were picked and the game was well underway, my entire team was in jail, which meant we were about to lose. I was the only one still free, and I was on my way to sneakily free them all when a thirteen-year-old boy spotted me making my move. There was about a hundred yards between me and the jail—a football field between victory and defeat. I began to sprint as fast as my little legs could go. Six years of track and hurdles were finally coming in handy!

Even so, I had underestimated the speed of my thirteen-year-old nemesis, who was closing in on me at an alarming pace. He was right on my tail, so I darted into the woods and weeds—a thicket, if you will—hoping to curtail the chase. Branches and brush began to pummel my face, but I really didn't notice because my people needed me to set them free. Their cheers propelled me forward. They were in sight. I could hear those pesky thirteen-year-old breaths behind me, which is much better than smelling them. I was so very close! Ten feet . . . five feet . . . two feet to go!

Freedom! I released the captives, and the game was won!

Sweat drenched my clothes as I put my hands on my knees, gulping air as fast as I could. As I looked down, I realized I had lost my shoe during the mad dash through the woods. The kids' reactions rivaled those inside an Olympic stadium after a gold medal has been won. It was a special moment—a special memory adding to the haven we wanted them to internalize.

Austin and Cody rushed off to find my shoe in the woods as if I was the champion of all champions and they were my humble servants. CJ's chest was puffed out among his peers, feeling proud of the prize recruit he had coaxed into playing.

After the boys were in bed and I had finally showered, I sat down for that coveted moment of stillness, but something was wrong with my eye. I must have gotten some speck of dust in it. I spent a lot of time trying to see what was in there with a magnifying glass, as did Dave when he got home, but we couldn't identify anything. I fell asleep exhausted, but happy.

The morning found me not nearly as happy. When I woke up, my eyelid was so swollen that I couldn't open it. The pain was almost unbearable. It felt as if a boulder had taken up residence just under my eyelid. It was gross, and there was no way I could avoid going to the eye doctor.

I sat in the darkened room as the ophthalmologist peered closely into my eye with his little black magnifying glass. I could feel his breath on my face, not my favorite part of going to the eye doctor. I could see concern on his face.

"What's wrong? Is it serious?"

"Well, this isn't something you see every day," he said as he straightened up and put down his scope.

Oh no, I thought. *It's probably some cancerous tumor that will kill me in three months, and Dave will be left to raise these three rapscallions alone!*

"What is it?" I asked timidly.

"You have a thorn in your eye that has lodged its way in fairly deep," he grimly pronounced. "I'm going to get the nurse. I'll have to remove it surgically."

I don't know how you feel about your eye, but the idea of touching my eyeball with something sharp was a terrifyingly unwelcome thought. Even so, the pain I was feeling was so bad that I was willing to get relief through almost any method.

Beyond that, I had an actual thorn in my eyeball! The apostle Paul described a thorn in his flesh, but in your eye? This was crazy. Nevertheless, I went home with my eye bandaged for the day and some eye drops to keep any infections at bay. The kids rushed into the house when my car pulled into the driveway, and I relayed all the gory details, which they reveled in.

Later that day, the screen door was open, and I could hear the older boys in the neighborhood asking CJ what had happened to my eye. "Oh, she got a thorn in her eye last night when we were playing capture the flag. She had to have surgery so the doctor could remove it." CJ said it in such a way that it sounded like the kind of thing that occurred every day in the Wilson house.

Through the screen, I could see the look of utter astonishment on his friends' faces. "Dude, your mom is awesome!" one exclaimed in a high-pitched voice. CJ smiled as though he'd known that truth for a long while now.

Yep, he was proud of his mom, who had almost killed herself running through the woods and had a patch over an eye filled with goo and swollen shut with grossness. I was proud to be this weird, misfit mom.

It may feel weird to be proud of being misfit parents, but we truly are. This is not just an issue of being extroverted or introverted. Some parents are quieter, some more creative, and some very competitive and outgoing. Even so, we all have one thing in common—the same thing most people in the world have in common: to desire to experience joy. This is something God has implanted in all our hearts.

Find out how you're made, and then build a haven out of your home that creates and preserves joy for your children, both in their present and in the memories they'll revisit in the future. Remember that this is not about comparisons—you may read what we did and think to yourself, *I could never do that stuff!* If our version doesn't resonate with you, it may be because this is simply not who you are.

Your job is to keep figuring out who you are so you can use the right tools that fit for your family to make your home a haven. It's not so much about what you are *doing*, but rather the atmosphere you are *creating*. If you enjoy something, your family will feed off of your passion.

And here's a friendly reminder: the greatest gift you can give to your kids is your presence. Modern technology brings both a beauty and a curse. We can be in the room with our kids, but we may not be engaged with them because we're preoccupied with our phones or tablets. Whether we realize it or not, the time and attention we offer is a reflection of what captures our hearts. Let your kids capture your heart more fully and consistently than your email, Facebook profile, or Instagram stories.

Trust God. Learn about yourself. Make memories. Build a haven. Spread joy.

Oh, and wear safety glasses while running through the woods.

— Reflections —

SECOND SON: AUSTIN

- If you find yourself constantly comparing your kids and your family to others on social media, take a break. Be real about your struggles and frustrations with social media by sharing with your spouse or trusted members of your real community. This can help break the comparison cycles that can happen in your social communities.
- Immediately stop reading and throw away the Christmas card from the family that lists their kids' incredible annual accomplishments.
- Work hard to never shame your kids (it can be harder work than you think). Definitely do not reference another child's accomplishments as a method or motivation to make your child less lazy, more well-behaved, or any other "less than" or "more than" that could affect your child's sense of worth.
- Build them up. Help them find what they're good at and discover the way God has uniquely wired them.
- If you hang a swing in the basement for your kids, make sure you hit the stud. The swing should be able to hold an adult. My dad missed the wood beam when he installed the swing in our basement and one of my kids got hurt—thanks, Dad.
- The minivan as a jet plane has definitely continued with my kids. This is how memories are made.
- Don't make your family an idol. If your kids rebel in their teen years, it's not all your fault. Continue to seek God and pray for your kids constantly.

CHAPTER 9

ON TARGET *with Teens*

Coaching Stage, Ages Twelve to Eighteen

You probably already have your own impression about "teens these days," as do I. Of all the stages in childhood, this coaching stage (ages twelve to eighteen) seems to cause more anxiety than any other, both during the years leading up to it and the years it takes place. In this society, we've given this season of life a host of negative labels, so it's no wonder that parents are nervous about it.

It is not uncommon to talk about teens as if they aren't really humans, but rather aliens who can't see the world as we do; can't control their impulses, behaviors, attitudes, or sexual desires; and ultimately can't be reasoned with until their hormones level out or the time of teenagedom finally and mercifully passes. Some of this perspective has merit. These can be very difficult years of physical change, social awkwardness, and transition into the scary waters of young adulthood. Even so, we don't think it's healthy to dread any season with your kids, nor is it healthy to concede that they are going to be stark raving mad for six or seven years, so we should just grit our teeth and accept it.

There are targets to aim at during these years. And God has much joy to offer as well, as you help your teens navigate this stage. In fact, the teen years were our favorite years of parenting. So we want to give you hope—and hope is a very important possession in all stages of life and parenting.

I (Dave) was once told an interesting story about teens by a high school baseball coach named Woody. On a Friday night in the spring, he and his wife went on a date in their small hometown in Ohio. After dinner and a movie, they retired early and were asleep by 10:00 p.m. Woody woke up around 2:00 a.m. and went downstairs to grab something to drink. He poured himself a glass of orange juice and walked into the family room to sit for a moment.

As he sat there, he noticed movement outside the sliding glass doors on his patio. He looked closer and saw a young teen boy standing just outside his door. He recognized the boy as the sophomore shortstop on his baseball team. Obviously, he wondered why the boy was standing outside his house at such an hour, especially since they were slated to have baseball practice at 8:00 a.m. that morning.

Woody began to chuckle as he told me the next part of the story. The boy had no idea that his baseball coach was watching him from only a few feet away when all of sudden, the kid began taking off his clothes. *All* of his clothes. Before Woody knew it, his shortstop was standing naked on his patio and was encouraging his other friends, also on the scene, to do the same. Once all of them were naked, the boys began running, chasing one another around the neighbor's house. Woody soon figured out that his next-door neighbor's daughter was hosting a sleepover. These boys had the bright idea of not only crashing the party but streaking the party.

As a high school baseball coach, Woody didn't seem to think this event was all that out of the ordinary. After all, he was around teens all the time—and you know teens are crazy, right?

I found out this same young man made other obvious lapses in judgment. Once he drove to a nightclub to engage in a lot of drinking and partying that left him far too impaired to drive home, but he did it anyway. In his infinite wisdom, he decided to take the back roads to avoid any run-ins with the police. His best friend was along for the ride. He had to stop about halfway home because of a train passing. The train took a long time to pass, so he put the car in park.

The next thing he knew, he and his buddy woke up in his car at 6:00 a.m.—they had fallen asleep there. His mother was beside herself, since she had no idea where her son was, and there were no cell phones back then. That boy Woody cared for so much was walking a dangerous path toward destruction. Yes, some of it was just "teen" stuff, but a lot of it was his attempt to make the leap into manhood without the influence of the most important man in his life—his father. This kid's single mom was terrified at how he was going to turn out.

You've probably figured out this teen boy was me. The choices I made when I first tasted the freedom of my teen years were scary. My mom said she stayed on her knees, constantly begging God to protect me and for Jesus to get ahold of my life. Thank God for praying moms! So before we even begin to delve into this stage, let me remind and encourage you that if you feel like abandoning hope that your teen will ever amount to anything good, trust me when I say that my mom thought the same thing. Don't give up. Hang in there, and go vertical daily because God just might do a miracle in your teen, like he did with me.

FROM TRAINING TO COACHING

The teen years can be a frightful time. As Ann and I walked through these years with our sons, we offered up many of the same desperate prayers all parents know well. I remember standing at the front window of our house as I watched our oldest, CJ, pull out of the driveway with his new driver's license in his pocket. I felt sheer terror in his newfound freedom. CJ had many great qualities, but driving in close quarters was not one of them. Before he left our nest, he had three wrecks . . . in our driveway! One night at a Bible study, we had some new visitors who were really nervous about coming to the pastor's house for a small group. As they timidly introduced themselves to us, we suddenly heard the sounds of CJ backing up and smashing our car directly into theirs in the driveway.

They had come nervous about doing Bible study with the pastor, but they should have come concerned about parking near the pastor's son's car in the driveway.

Yet with all the negative press surrounding these years, when we look back at them now, we think of them as our favorites. I know that sounds crazy, but be encouraged. Yes, these years were filled with all kinds of scary and challenging moments, but Ann and I absolutely cherished the time we had with our sons who were becoming men. And obviously, we don't have any daughters, but Ann will continue to share a female perspective about this season for young women as well.

During our time in this coaching stage, we learned a lot about what makes a teen tick and what parenting looks like during this time—and a lot of it was by doing the wrong thing. That's bad news for us, but good news for you, because this means you get to learn from our mistakes. Perhaps you won't have to repeat them in your home to get the lesson into your heart.

These are the years when we become more like coaches to our kids than nurses, teachers, short-order cooks (this one may still apply), or hall monitors. In this stage, our kids don't want us or often need us—believe it or not—to tell them every little thing to do or every little choice to make. If we do this—that is, fail to recognize the differences in this stage from the previous ones—we can make them feel smothered.

Trust me, we failed here plenty of times. It's natural to want to keep intervening as you always have, but we had to learn to know when to take a step back and give them some freedom to make their own decisions. The hope is that the discipline and training we poured into them for the first twelve years will begin paying off now. And even if it seems to remain incognito for a while during this stage, don't give up. This is a long game.

Oddly enough, all teens tend to develop an addiction that manifests right around the age of twelve or thirteen, perhaps even younger if puberty hits early. Do you know what they are addicted to? No, it's not their phones, social media, food, or porn—although all of these can definitely happen. Above all of these things, almost universally, teens have an almost uncontrollable desire for *freedom*.

We should remember that for much of world history, they would have been considered adults in their early teens. It was common for teens to take jobs, get married, have kids, work the fields, or even go to war. Obviously, this is one area where we believe the modern perspective is better than the old one. There are some things that kids have no business doing at such a tender age.

However, these historical perspectives reveal an interesting fact: teens really didn't exist before the last two centuries or so. There were kids and there were young adults, but there was no middle ground. Today, the whole world acknowledges the teen years as a special season with its own set of rules and expectations.

This reality has positives and negatives. Positively, these years give kids more time to mature at a healthy pace before they fully enter the world. It also prevents abusive practices such as kids being married off at young ages or being forced to work dangerous jobs. The negative side is this: teens sometimes think they get a pass on life for about eight years or so. It's as if we've confirmed that they are incapable of making good decisions during these years, and we say things like, "Well, he was a teenager, and you know they're all crazy!" A wiser approach is somewhere in between, where teens are not crushed by the full weight of an adult world, yet are also not given a license to run amok.

The truth is, their growth into adults is happening quickly during these years, yet they still have underdeveloped bodies and underdeveloped frontal lobes in their brains. The frontal lobe is only the center for impulse control and for one's judgment of consequences—so yeah, nothing could go wrong here! Indeed, their brains will often try to convince them to make stupid decisions as they taste their first years of freedom. We need to be empathetic and compassionate to their teen plight. But we shouldn't let them dodge responsibility by saying, "My teen brain made me do it!"

For the first twelve years of our children's lives, we've been telling them what to think and what to believe. We have set our values to be their values. We have dictated that our priorities are their priorities. But now they will begin to question—or, rather, to test—all of these things for themselves. They need a coach. They need you. They need adults who will guide them through this season. They also need you to become a little thicker-skinned, because this isn't easy for them, just as it wasn't easy for you. (Take it from a recovering streaker—no one is proud of everything that happened when they were a teen.)

We shouldn't be surprised when our middle schooler wants us to drop him off a block, or a mile, from the school so he doesn't have to be seen with us. This is perfectly normal for this season because they are becoming adults and tasting freedom for the first time. As they begin to inch away from us and into adulthood, where they will make choices on their own, they will do some stupid things—and they will pay for it. Remember that bad choices yield bad consequences. I was kicked off the baseball team for a time and lost my driving privileges for several months.

This is a season when parents will do their kids no favors by bypassing or removing these consequences. This is how they learn, so we have to let them learn—even when it hurts them and us.

I love how Shaunti Feldhahn and Lisa Rice describe this stage in their book *For Parents Only.*[1] They say that parents have spent years building a castle, constructing it block by block. These blocks are our values, beliefs, priorities, and the like. We have instilled these blocks into our children, stacking them day to day with our experiences, words, impressions, and discipline. For the most part, our kids have accepted these values as fact for their entire lives.

But now, they will begin to challenge these core values. They will pick up each block and question whether they also want to build their own lives with this particular block. They pick up the block called "sexual purity," look at it, and say, "Do I believe this? Do I want to live my life this way?" They will pick

1. Shaunti Feldhahn and Lisa A. Rice, *For Parents Only: Getting Inside the Head of Your Kid* (Colorado Springs: Multnomah, 2007), 45–52. By the way, *For Parents Only* is the best book we've read on the topic of parenting teens.

up the block called "avoiding harmful drugs and the abuse of alcohol" and begin weighing whether this one will make it into the structure of their own lives. Integrity. Faith. Relationships. They are all blocks you've stacked, but now they will be unstacked and examined by the very ones you have spent so many years building this wall of love and protection around.

This deconstruction can feel like rejection, but I encourage you to not freak out and begin dropping these blocks on them in frustration. The deconstruction is natural and necessary. If the blocks you have built the family with are strong and trustworthy, your children will begin using them to build their own lives as well. There is no way to bypass this deconstruction. You can't and shouldn't want to force them into building with your blocks. You simply provide the raw material.

They will build their own lives with whatever blocks they decide to use, just as you did. You will sometimes feel shocked by some of their choices. The key is to not freak out in front of them after a bad choice. You can freak out later with your spouse or with a friend. "Can you believe she just colored her hair purple?" Though honestly, if hair color is your biggest issue, you may consider just being supportive and falling to your knees later in gratitude to God. But with your teens, if you make their desire to make choices for themselves a bloody battleground where every inch of every issue is a fight, just know you may end up as one of the casualties.

With teens, we need to live life with them by "living in the question." We should always ask questions that invite them into the decision process of their own freedom, a process that will soon be completely up to them anyway. For the first twelve or so years of our children's lives, we've told them what to think, but now we need to constantly be asking them, "What do *you* think?"

What do you think about that R-rated movie?

What do you think about hanging out with those kids?

What do you think about looking at porn?

Of course, we must still know when to lay down the law firmly for our teens, but we also need to allow them to be heard. At the teen stage, the words "because I said so" no longer work. Your kids will often push back on such expressions, which is why it's good to ask questions that will lead them to their own understanding of what's right rather than to just rote knowledge or regurgitation of a viewpoint they may not be ready to adopt for themselves just yet. Instead of "I told you so," try, "So what do you think is the proper decision in this circumstance? And why do you think that?"

This is a balancing act that produces tension. The best practice is not to try to end this tension, but rather to keep living in it so it can produce both safety and healthy autonomy for them. The harder we jam our values down their throats at this stage, the more likely they are to reject those values. They are longing for the freedom to make their own choices.

Don't freak out. They will often choose to live out the same values you have built into their lives. This is great when it happens, but they will still want to make these decisions for themselves, even when it comes to your shared values. While they want freedom, rules and boundaries help them avoid becoming overwhelmed by the vastness of the adult experience. They will push harder against the boundaries you establish. So try not to be shocked when they slam into (and through) some of them. I remember a particular night when our family was eating at the dinner table. (This is something we recommend for every family at every stage. Sports and extracurricular activities make us all crazy busy, but prioritizing eating dinner together as a family yields more dividends than you might think.)

Our boys were teens at the time, and Ann asked them, "What do we do as parents that really bugs you? What rules do you think are stupid?"

CJ was seventeen at the time. He said, "I think it's stupid to make me go to bed so early. I'm old enough to stay up later because I can do fine now with less sleep." We listened to him, and after some thought, we both agreed he was mature enough, so we relaxed that standard.

He must have really felt the rush of his freedom, because then he pushed further and said, "And I also think it's really dumb that I can't have my girlfriend over here when you guys aren't home." Ah, there it is—the tension of knowing what freedoms to *grant* and what restrictions should not be *taken for granted.* We didn't budge on this one, because no matter how he felt about it, he wasn't equipped for this—just as I wouldn't have been equipped for it at his age. The rule remained: no girls in the house when Mom and Dad aren't around.

He reluctantly agreed to obey this rule, but we hoped he had felt heard because we were "living in the question." He was old enough to not just be told what to do, but we were also able to explain why this value was important for our family, one we hoped he would carry with him when his time came to choose the building blocks of his own life.

And guess what? He did—and today his wife is glad he did.

THE KEY TO YOUR TEEN

The key to raising great teens (not perfect ones, but ones who see the value of your building blocks and may choose to use some of them in their own adulthood) comes down to one key word: *relationship.* Even though they are instinctively pulling away, deep down they still need—and want—a relationship with their parents. They usually won't tell you this. In fact, everything about them can feel like it's screaming that they don't want you in their lives, but they really do, especially in the ways that help you both feel safe, heard, and loved.

Many parents feel discouraged when their teens pull away, so they basically give up on having a relationship with them. We get it, but we encourage you to avoid taking everything they say or don't say to heart. They are in transition, so everything feels unsettled. You can rest assured that who they are now is not who they will end up becoming, so don't create patterns or make decisions now as if you're dealing with their fully developed versions. Don't demolish a road that is still under construction just because it gets a little bumpy. That's what roads under construction feel like. Stay on it, knowing that it's a work in progress. This road leads somewhere you really want to go—into loving relationships with your kids in their adulthood.

Don't give up as they slowly walk away. I know that every inch they take feels like a mile of separation to you. Try to fight harder against the offense and pain you feel within yourself than you fight against the daily onslaught of changes happening within them. Seek to find relational balance, because this is a critical time to *build* this relationship, not wound it, trap it, or end it.

Ann has already mentioned it, but the following statement still rings so very true during this season of parenting: *Rules without relationships lead to rebellions.* If all we do in our kids' teen lives is constantly lay down more and more rules but have no real relationship with them, there's a high probability they will rebel against those rules. This isn't guaranteed, but even in your own life, it's much easier to obey someone you love and who you know loves you in return. God is Exhibit A.

It's also much easier when you actually *like* each other. You can't always guarantee that through the difficult moments of this stage "liking" will be easy. You'll often not at all like what your teens are saying or trying to do. But try to always look past their behavior to remember their value and uniqueness. The things you've always liked about them are still in there somewhere. Don't throw them out because you're frustrated. You will not always be their best friend during these years, but you also shouldn't approach this stage as though it's a warden-inmate situation. Keep loving them, but keep striving to like them as well.

So how do we build a great relationship with our teens? Here are some thoughts.

Pursue. Pursue. Pursue.

Don't retreat when they pull away. Instead, pursue them like never before. Don't smother them, but don't abandon them. They are trying to discover who they are—their identity—and you are a big part of that, even if you sometimes feel like the unwelcome part. They may very well tell you to butt out of their lives, but don't believe their words. Instead, find creative ways to keep spending time with them.

Dads, if you have a daughter, take her out on a daddy-daughter date regularly. Make plans, complete with reservations at the restaurant. Dress up a bit. Clean the car and pull it around, and then ring the front doorbell. Take her out, open all the doors, and ask her questions. Create a beautiful evening that honors your daughter. Above all else, spend a lot of time listening. Don't be afraid to let her into your life too. Be her dad but also her friend—this is the age when this friendship can begin to be fostered and developed. I don't have a daughter, but after a lifetime in ministry and many friends with daughters,

I can tell you that if you are intentional and relational, these years can be a precious time for a teen daughter and her dad.

Another word here about teen daughters (although many books have been written on the subject). So much of a dad's role during these years is to support, protect, and reinforce in a relationally safe way. I advise against a lot of the distance and bravado that many dads show when their daughters begin to become young women. Men tend to shy away or suddenly want to act like every moment signals the chance to polish their shotgun in front of any boys who come near. While protecting her physically is a given, loving her with gentleness, understanding, patience, and engagement is the way you will protect not only her physical well-being but also her emotional well-being—as well as your relationship with her. Some of the changes in her life may make you uncomfortable, but be careful not to put undue distance between you and her over it. To do so will only lead her to feel shame and insecurity.

A huge part of this role also includes nourishing the relationship between your teen daughter and her mother. Her mom will be the woman who walks with her through all of the changes you are helpless to address. Even so, a sense of resentment and even enmity between teen daughters and their moms often arises. It may well be simply a manifestation of many other tensions in everyone's life during these years of transition, but it can do a lot of damage in moments when they should be on the same side.

Avoid the temptation to retreat into "this is girls' stuff" territory, which can allow you to be the bystander or even the "good guy" your daughter runs to in order to escape the perceived tyranny of her mother. In this moment, always offer comfort, but never to the detriment of your solidarity as a parenting team. Since this stage involves a lot of talking and questions, ask questions that will help your daughter reengage and stay relationally connected to the most important woman in her life at one of the most formative moments in her life. Many hurts are caused, some that can echo for years, between mothers and daughters because dads were passive during these conflicts. Dads, engage and be a helpful part of that conversation.

You can support your daughter without corroborating destructive patterns. Yes, Mom will be wrong sometimes, just as Dad will be wrong sometimes. Keep the target of a sound relationship at the center of these conflicts, preserving this value above the tug-of-war for freedom your daughter is experiencing. Keep looking ahead a few years to a time when teen hormones have leveled out, your kid has a household of her own, and the bridge of joyful sharing, support, and friendship between mother and daughter still stands because even when it threatened to be blown up, Dad kept gently engaging to defuse these bombs.

Moving to sons, an area we have a little more experience in, it is obvious that you can't take your sons on dates—not even moms. Trust me, that will *not* be cool. The alternative is to "hang" with them. This is actually the same thing as a date—so just don't call it that. We began some of these traditions when the boys were young. I would take all of them out of the house together for one day each month to give Ann a break. We called it "Boys Day Out," and it became an epic day for us as guys. These days almost always involved A&W root beer floats and hanging at an arcade. The boys looked forward to Boys Day Out each month, as did their dad.

But when they reached their teen years and I'd say, "Hey, let's go hang," they would usually have something better to do with their friends. Sure, this was hard on good old dad. I really like root beer floats with my guys. These moments can tempt you to just give up and stop worrying about this quality time, but I urge you to resist that temptation. *Don't give up; get creative.*

I knew each of our boys was wired differently, so I pursued time with each of them according to their interests.

"Hey, CJ, you want to go to Best Buy?" The answer was almost always yes. He loves tech stuff.

"Hey, Austin, you want to go on an adventure?" He'd be putting on his boots before I finished the question.

"Hey, Cody, you want to go throw the football?" Forget boots—he'd have his cleats on and be outside waiting for me.

Obviously, these respective interests aren't at all what defined each of my sons, but they did offer me clues to positive ways to pursue them. Those times were precious because during the teen years, the calendar gets packed with many other things. Time with Mom or Dad will get lost unless we intentionally make it happen.

Ann was vigilant about pursuing these kinds of moments with our teen sons. She was adamant about taking a family vacation together every year. I would object on the grounds that it cost too much, but Ann wouldn't take no for an answer. I won't say who won these battles. I will only say we went on vacation every single year. (Masculinity intact.) Looking back, I'm so glad we did. I also think these vacations are some of our kids' favorite memories as a family.

One vivid memory involves driving twenty-four hours to Naples, Florida, in our minivan on a trip arranged by Ann. The best part was that we were given free lodging at a friend's condo. It should go without saying that a drive that long with three boys of that age (oh, and a dog too) was exhausting. I still get tired when I think about it.

The truth is, everyone complained and yelled at each other

most of the long trip down and back. Also, we got lost. This was back in the days when we still used maps like Marco Polo (the explorer, not the pool game). Someone threw up. Mom and Dad fought over the directions, and the map got sucked (or thrown, depending on which side of the story you believe) out the window. Oh, yeah, and Mr. Tech son (CJ) filmed the whole ordeal, and the video evidence remains to this day.

But do you know what I remember the most? Sitting outside with my family, watching them banter back and forth as they made s'mores over a campfire. In that moment, I became aware that I was the most blessed man in all the world. Those memories are precious now, but if we would have succumbed to the complaints and protests of our teen boys, we would have never made the trip. Thank God for a wife and mom like Ann, who understood how important it is to pursue time with our kids.

There are countless ways to do it, but here's a quick list of some ideas for pursuing your teens:

- Get home. Love is spelled T.I.M.E.
- Eat dinner together.
- Listen to their music.
- Watch their videos with them.
- Read what they are reading.
- Question what they are questioning—especially regarding their faith.
- Text them.
- Get to know their friends. (I was a failure at this, and I regret it.)
- Get food out. (They love to eat, and when they eat, they will talk.)
- Stay up late, because they are up and that's when they will talk. (You can sleep when they're gone!)

Listen. Listen. Listen.

One of the most common complaints (usually the biggest) teens have about their parents is that they don't listen. When we stop listening, they will shut down and instead turn to their friends or other outlets to express what's going on inside of them. It's completely normal for our teens to turn to their friends as their primary source of wisdom during this stage, but we all know that their friends are in the same boat as they are, so their wisdom is limited, even if their intentions are pure. There will be many moments when they need and even long for an adult perspective. If we are present and willing to listen, they will talk to us.

In Feldhahn and Rice's research with teens, they made this discovery: "Eight out of ten kids—both boys and girls—said that instead of wanting parents to jump in and fix a problem, they first needed parents to hear, acknowledge, and tend to the emotions behind the problem."[2]

I believe that deep down, our teens are longing to be seen and accepted both for who they are and for who they are becoming. They want to be loved as they are. As their parents, we know we *do* love them for who they are, but we're also trying to help them become the person they need to become. Listening is the bridge across this tension. Ironically, when we listen instead of always having to talk, we are saying something very important to our teens: "You are valuable to me, and I love you." When we simply cut them off with answers and rules, they feel unheard and unseen. Rebellion, isolation, and emotional distancing from one's parents is often a result of being unheard by them.

I hate to admit it, but I did a very poor job of living out this

2. Feldhahn and Rice, *For Parents Only*, 117.

truth with our boys. Looking back, I realize I was consumed with my job and that all too often I was not home. I wasn't there to hear what my teen sons were saying. As a pastor, it was much easier to share my heart from the stage with my congregation than to intimately share my heart in our family room with my own sons. They heard me tell personal stories and express emotions in sermons—stories and emotions I seldom shared with them in the privacy of our own home. My failing to do this was a violation of their trust, and it made them feel like the church was more important to me than they were. I know this now because, as adult men, they have loved me well enough to tell me. It was crushing to hear this from my grown sons, but I needed to hear it.

I share it with you so you can avoid my mistake.

Share your heart with your teen son or daughter, but always remember to listen for their hearts as well. I missed out, but you don't have to. Learn from my failures. It is never too late. We can work on it now, even though the teen years may have passed. Going vertical with repentance and change means that God will continue to redeem things that are unredeemable by human efforts. We need something *supernatural* because our natural means are less than super.

Listening isn't easy. I may not have listened as well as I should have, but I was still graced with some important conversations during this season. I remember one evening as CJ was crawling into bed, he commented that he didn't understand how God could condemn murder in the Ten Commandments and yet condone all of the other acts of killing in the Old Testament. I could tell that Ann was ready to freak out because our middle school son was questioning God and the Bible. As I listened to his comment, I knew he was beginning to wrestle with his faith—to examine the blocks. We must all wrestle with our faith, because at some point, it needs to become *our* faith, not just *their* faith. I did the same in my teen years, and I still question my faith at times today. I was familiar with the journey CJ was on, so I looked at him and said, "Now that's a great question. I've wondered the same thing. How can that make sense, CJ?"

Ann looked at me as if I had lost my mind, but I knew that if we rejected this question, we would also be rejecting any answers. We also might not be invited to join him on any pathways of thought and growth he would walk in the years to come. He wouldn't feel safe to ask questions like these in our presence. He would rightly need to get his answers from someone else—and who knew where that could lead.

If you are especially strong in your faith, this can make you feel weak and out of control. But it is a part of the process. Many parents forfeit their rights to be present on the intellectual journey toward faith with their kids at the very moment this journey matters the most because they don't allow the process to occur. If your teens question their faith, don't freak out. They are asking you to examine the blocks with them. Even if they are sacred topics, realize that their honesty and courage to invite you in is also a sacred act. Don't miss the forest for the trees.

I still enjoy discussing the deeper issues of faith with CJ, Austin, and Cody. We don't agree on all aspects of theology, but I think they feel the freedom to push back on us and yet remain confident they are still loved and accepted, even when we don't agree. I hope their comments in this book reflect this perspective. We shall see.

Remember our bull's-eye? *Train and launch L3 warriors [Love/Lock/Live] who make a dent where they are sent.* Obviously, passing on our faith remains a huge goal for us as parents.

We probably pray about this as much as anything for our kids. So how does this goal reconcile with this seemingly nonchalant acceptance of their questioning? Well, Christian parents tend to think the best way to help our kids develop their faith is to get them to church and in the youth group. While I agree that these are helpful and important strategies, there is something that is way more important—something that affects this process at an exponentially higher rate.

Model. Model. Model.

As a parent, *how you live out* your faith is more important than how well you get your teens plugged in to a youth group. We have a thriving youth ministry at our church that is doing amazing things with our teens. Take it from someone who has been observing these kinds of things for more than thirty years: When the teens in our church don't see the faith they hear about at church being lived out by their parents, this faith doesn't resonate with them or last through their young adult years in the same way. Conversely, those students who came up through our youth ministries and who seem to be living out a vibrant faith are predominantly kids who grew up in homes where moms and dads modeled what a vibrant faith looks like. Obviously, there are always exceptions, but the trend is undeniable. Our kids are watching us like hawks, and at some point they will copy what they see, even if only parts of it. And the most important part is that your journey with Christ is real, authentic, full of repentance, open to doubts and questioning, and a daily element of your life that continually brings change to your attitudes and actions.

Your faith doesn't need to be perfect. Those parents who believe their faith is an example of perfection are in reality modeling something harmful for their kids—either judgmental self-righteousness or an unattainable version of perfection that will lead them to give up and stop trying. Both are harmful, and honestly, the first may be more harmful than the second.

The truth is, I sin and you sin—and our kids are watching us 24-7. We can't live flawless lives, but we can honor a flawless Savior we keep bringing our brokenness to. We can admit it and apologize when we blow it. Our teens shouldn't expect us to not make mistakes or to live sinless lives, so even if they want to see us in this light, keep bringing yourself down a peg in their eyes. Otherwise, when they're old enough to figure out that you don't have it all together, they will see your sinfulness as a broken promise about what being a Christian means. The truth is, they should know from the get-go that sinfulness is universal, even among their parents. Only Jesus lived a sinless life, which is why we all equally need him. An authentic Christ follower doesn't get everything right. They know how to keep growing in the righteousness that is freely bestowed on redeemed sinners by the only One who actually has it to give. Don't inadvertently teach them a false gospel based on your goodness instead of Christ's. Trust us, this will be a block they will eventually and rightly examine and discard because it is severely cracked and unstable.

To model Christianity for your kids is to model authenticity, a lifestyle of learning and confession. To acknowledge that goodness doesn't come from all your good behavior but from the only One who is good.

Cody once came home from college for winter break after playing in a college football bowl game. He was off for a week, something quite rare for college athletes. I asked him if he would help me preach my sermon that weekend at church, and he agreed. His faith was strong, and he did an amazing job.

It was obvious that he had a gift, and now, ten years later, he is an effective communicator, and we work together in ministry.

But back then, he was still young in his own adult faith. After this sermon we delivered together, a men's group from our church asked me if I would join them for dinner at a local retreat they were hosting. They wanted an hour or so to ask some "dad questions." They also asked if Cody could join us. I thought it was a great idea to hear from a father and a son. At one point, one of the dads said, "Cody, it's clear from your sermon on Sunday that you have a strong, vibrant faith. What did your dad do to help stoke that fire?"

When I heard the question, I remember thinking how hard it would be for Cody to answer it. After all, I had done *so many* great things. Would it be the many Bible studies I had led him through? Would it be the amazing sermons he had heard me preach weekly for decades? Would it be the mission trips we went on together? Would it be the "rite of passage" trip we took when he was thirteen years old? There were so many great options to choose from that I knew it would be tough to narrow it down to a single thing.

But to my surprise, Cody just sat there. He didn't have an immediate answer, which sort of fed my "too much good to narrow it down" narrative but also made me nervous. He sat silent for so long that it became awkward. This wasn't good.

Finally he said, "I really don't remember any of the words Dad said. And I don't really remember any of the Bible studies he did with me. Most of those were sort of boring." This couldn't have been going any better.

"In fact, I can only think of one thing he did that helped me develop my fire for Jesus: he lived it. If I ever wanted to know what a real man of God looked like, he was right down the hall."

This is not a pat on the back for me. It just shows I was so very wrong about most things. Being willing to be wrong in front of him was more powerful than I realized. Living out of this perspective may wound our pride as parents, but let it be slain! There is too much at stake. Live a life of faith in front of them with all of its messiness. All the other stuff is icing on the cake. Your life and how you live your faith are what they will carry out of your home—or what they will leave at the doorstep.

I blew it many times. You have too. Maybe you read this with tears in your eyes because, like me, you didn't live in authentic brokenness, and now your kids in their adulthood seem to have rejected the block of your faith. Let me encourage you—it's never too late to be broken and honest. Start now. Acknowledge your mistakes, and begin exploring what your faith is based on. Is it your own goodness, or is it the radical grace of Christ? Begin admitting faults now that they never heard when they lived under your roof.

You may have blown it then, but you don't have to blow it now. Go vertical, and see what God can do to redeem and restore what all of us have broken. Cultivate an authentic walk with God now. If you're reading this, you're still breathing. Your legacy isn't yet fully decided. Your mistakes may be unchangeable, but your heart is not.

It's never too late, so start right here, right now.

CHAPTER 10

PUSHING DOWN AND *Pulling Away*

A Mom's Perspective

"Guys, *come on*, we're late!" I (Ann) had yelled because I knew they probably couldn't hear me above the sound of the video game they were supposed to have shut off ten minutes ago when I yelled the first time.

Dave was packing food in the car for the gathering with friends we were headed to. Periodically, a bunch of us would gather our families for food and fun. It was a cold but beautiful Michigan winter day. Our friends had an ice-skating pond by their house that they had shoveled off for what promised to be a spectacular day of memory making. Great food, fun, bonfires, and s'mores. It doesn't get much better than that in February in Michigan!

I could still hear the rumble of the video game. I trudged into the house, frustrated, since this was now the fourth time I had called them. They knew the plan. "Come on!" I stomped down the stairs loudly on purpose so they'd know I meant business.

Good try, Ann. I told myself. *They wouldn't hear you if a freight train was barreling through the room.* Their eyes were glued to the screen.

"Guys, we're done!" I said, as I turned off the TV.

"*Mom!* We weren't done yet!" CJ yelled as he stood up.

He was almost a foot taller than me now, and at fourteen years old, he was already as big as his dad. I looked up at him, trying to be nonchalant and keep my composure.

"It's time to go," I calmly declared.

Inside my mind, I congratulated myself for keeping my composure. Those parenting books I'd been reading on teens were really paying off. Calm and Cool—that was my new middle name.

Twelve-year-old Austin and nine-year-old Cody raced each other up the stairs to get their coats. CJ pounded each step with his size-eleven foot, making sure I knew he was disgusted with me and the whole thing.

"Whatever, dude!" I said. "You can huff and puff all you want, but you aren't shaking my good mood and this great day."

The day was everything we had anticipated. Crisp air, a bright blue sky, ice-skating with so many great friends, and great conversations as the moms huddled around the fire. The sun was going down, and hunger pangs were setting in. Some of the parents had already gone in to set up food for our hungry horde. There were probably about ten families gathered, with twenty-five or more kids between the ages of four to eighteen.

Yes, it was utter chaos.

These were all church families we had known at Kensington from the early years of the church's existence. Each family huddled together and quieted down because they knew someone would pray and then give instructions about going through the food line. Austin and Cody joined Dave and me, but when I looked for CJ, my eyes found him checking out the food tables. He looked up, and I motioned for him to come join us.

The room was quiet and the host was about to pray, but someone's voice broke the silence. "This food looks like crap!" a male voice blurted out. Giggling, groans, astonishment, and awkwardness filled the room . . . and it sucked the air out of my body because it was apparent that my son, I mean, *Dave's* son, had mumbled these mortifying words.

"CJ!" I heatedly whispered close to his ear. "Stop it. What a horrible and rude thing to say!"

"Why? It's true!" he proclaimed in a voice much louder than my whisper.

I was humiliated beyond words. What would people think of us as parents? I could feel myself turning red. Thankfully, someone prayed, and I'm not even sure what happened the rest of the night—that is, until we began getting ready to leave.

We were trying to gather our scattered snow gear, leftover food, and coats. Most people were still hanging out, talking or playing games. I asked Cody where his boots were, but he told me he had worn only his ice skates. I found that hard to believe, but such is life with nine-year-olds. Finally, it appeared we were ready to walk out the door. Dave was still gathering things, so I turned to CJ next to me.

"CJ, will you carry Cody out to the car? He forgot to bring his boots. Just give him a piggyback ride to the car."

"What the heck, Mom! I have to do *everything* around here!"

Once again, the entire room was suddenly enveloped in silence as all eyes peered at the "godly" Wilson family making their less than subtle departure. I gave CJ the stink eye, trying to communicate how much trouble he was about to be in. Again, mortified, I sheepishly said my goodbyes. Austin went out the door first, quickly complying and well aware of my anger and embarrassment. CJ was right behind Austin, and I was right behind CJ, about as close as I could get to make sure he could hear every word that came out of my mouth.

"You are in so much trouble!" I began my tirade. "You were rude, insensitive, insolent, and a downright brat! You should know better at fourteen years old. And if I ask you to do something, you should do it with no questions asked. Do you have any idea how much I do for you? That was so embarrassing!"

As we got to the car, I opened the car door since CJ had Cody on his back. Austin was already in the car, seat belt fastened. CJ turned sideways and bent over into an awkward position, trying to get Cody off his back without hitting his or Cody's head. Cody climbed off, but CJ was off balance as his weight shifted.

In a split second, something happened within me. I watched as CJ struggled with his balance. I saw a huge snowbank right behind him. I instinctively nudged him with my shoulder, which was all it took in his awkward position to send him careening straight into the snowbank. His arms and legs were flailing haphazardly as snow covered his body and face.

I wasn't done though. If he was going to act like a foolish teen, then so was I. I quickly slammed Cody's car door, opened my car door, and jumped into the passenger seat just in time to lock all the doors. It was a masterful move that no one expected, but these were desperate times.

CJ clambered out of the snowbank and stepped over to the car door, only to find it locked. He began pounding on the window. "Let me in!"

Now the stink eye was fired toward my backseat passengers, along with a growl. "Don't you dare unlock that door!" Now the family was finally in compliance, just like I had drawn it up. A minute later, Dave arrived at the car and opened the tailgate to begin loading the dishes into the car.

"CJ, what are you doing?" He calmly asked. "Get in the car."

I quickly hit the unlock button, and CJ got in the car.

Silence.

Dave broke the silence. "Uh, guys? What's going on?"

Floodgates opened.

"*Mom* pushed me into a snowbank and then locked me out of the car!" CJ accusingly pronounced.

Pastor Dave gave me a little side-glance, curiously inquiring with his eyes if such a preposterous story could actually be true.

"Yes, I did it!" I blurted out, confessing my crime as if I was on trial. "But it wasn't a push; it was just a nudge."

I think that was when I heard the words come out of my mouth, as though I was watching a train wreck I couldn't turn away from. In this case, I was the conductor. Guilt suddenly overtook me.

"I want you to know, Dave, I will *never* teach on parenting with you onstage because I have no idea what I'm doing!" It wasn't just about the Snowbank Incident, as it came to be known in the annals of Wilson family folklore; it was about CJ's horrible behavior from start to finish, a monument to my failings as a mother. All was lost.

"And I'm sorry, CJ," I confessed. "I shouldn't have *nudged* you into the snowbank." And with that, the tears started to flow. Yes, I was mad at myself for my (mostly) uncalled-for actions, and I was frustrated with CJ for his rudeness, but I was angry that I cared so much what other people thought of me and my parenting skills. I didn't think people's opinions meant that much to me, but I realized in that moment just how much they really did.

Isn't that what parenting does? It exposes all of our weaknesses, insecurities, and frailties. This happens the most in the early years and in the teen years—the discipline stage and the coaching stage. Even so, the teen years turned out to be one of my favorite seasons. I was a mess with CJ (poor guy), but I got a little better as we went along together. I only had to push him into a few more snowbanks to get there.

I'm kidding . . . mostly.

COMMUNICATING IN THE CHAOS

I must admit that there are better ways to communicate than burying your loved one in snow. We may not have had our finest hour on that particular day, but one of my favorite things about CJ is that he has always been true to himself. He speaks frankly and honestly, refusing to use his words flippantly. And it's still the case as an adult, but maturity has helped him to be more thoughtful before he speaks and to measure his actions and his words.

Again, he came by his teenage spontaneous combustion honestly. See previous story.

CJ is a highly intelligent thinker and problem solver. He's laid-back and easily goes with the flow, but during those teen years, he was simply learning how to say things that were truthful without hurting people's feelings. We all need grace, but this is especially true for teens who are figuring out life and who they are.

Yes, we all need grace, but parents are often the first ones to withhold it from other parents and from themselves. As you can see, I'm passionate and bold. I'm a thinker and a truth-teller, just like my son. I'm still learning what to say and how to say it. I've since learned to pause more before I speak or take action—to wait before I push, as it were. Jesus has helped me with this. CJ, Austin, Cody, and Dave have helped too.

But all of this helping is complicated and sometimes painful, as are most processes of positive personal growth. In fact, the teen years can become a time of grieving for us parents. It can feel like we're losing those little innocent souls who used to want to cuddle with us and listen to us. It's the time in life where the window of our influence is closing and the window of their peers' influence is opening faster than we wish. They used to look to us for their approval, but now they're beginning to look to their friends instead. It's sad, but some of it is necessary.

When Austin hit his teen years, he became much quieter and more reserved. I didn't know what was going on in his head, so I'd ask him a ton of questions. I just wanted to know what he was thinking and who he was becoming. I knew my inquisitions bugged him, but I didn't know what else to do. Despite the annoyance, Austin was naturally gentler and seldom said things to intentionally hurt my feelings. I may have never pushed him into the snow, but it still felt like he was slipping away into his own world.

Cody was a bit more transparent in his experience. His love language was touch, so when he was younger, he would beg me or Dave to get under the blanket with him when we read to him at bedtime. We were always more than happy to oblige.

But I'll never forget the night I lifted the covers to lie down to talk with him before our prayers, and he said, "What are you doing?" His voice was suddenly accusatory, as if I was some stranger he had just met on the street.

"I was just getting under the blanket to pray for you," I said innocently.

"Get out of here, Mom!"

And with that, I slunk out of the room and into the hallway to sit on the floor. Dave had just come upstairs to say good night to Cody. "Why are you sitting here?" he asked.

"It has finally begun with Cody," I told him sadly. "My window with him has closed."

I was sad when each one entered this point in their lives, but I didn't realize that some of the best moments of parenting still lay ahead. The best conversations, the most laughs, the biggest fights, the discovery of who God had made them to be—it all lay ahead. It was a lot, and it ran the gamut of emotions, but we didn't want to miss all the beauty in the deluge of changes.

Thus our motto during those days became, *Don't take it personally*.

You probably already know a lot of what I'm about to say, but bear with me anyway. This isn't always a matter of knowledge, but a matter of perspective, recollection, and encouragement. Teens' brains are growing; their hormones are going crazy; their bodies are growing and changing like never before; and they don't know what to think of themselves, let alone us. So take a breath, because it's going to be okay. And it will be the ride of your life. And so, how about a couple of tips for the road.

Tip #1: Don't Pull Away

I know Dave already discussed this, but it's worth another mention. Why? Because when your kids seemingly reject you, pulling away from you over and over again, the natural reaction is to give them what they want and pull away in return. It feels like they don't want us at times. They say mean and hurtful things that can make us want to either cry in our closets or buy a hockey mask and go to war—and these are not gender-specific reactions.

Teens may act confident and sure of themselves, but deep down inside, they are often racked with fear and anxiety as their peers' opinions begin to matter more and more. You will find yourself having to get on them all the time because suddenly they are sleeping and eating more, while also seemingly growing lazier, messier, and more selfish.

But I'll remind you of what Dave has already told us: Our job as parents is to *pursue* our teens. Don't expect them to initiate. *You* initiate. I'm the first to admit how hard this is when they seem to prefer anything and everything over you—including, but not limited to, friends, video games, social media, the dog, and their favorite bar of soap (okay, that last one was weird). Pursue them anyway. Your *selflessness* will continue to combat their *selfishness*. Keep being the right kind of grown-up, even when they think they are already grown-ups. Keep modeling. Keep pursuing.

Sidebar: A word to dads and their daughters. Dave wrote about this from the male perspective of his friends who have daughters, but let me address it as a daughter myself. Dads, I know this can be an awkward time for you. Your daughter is becoming a woman, and you may feel like you don't know how to proceed. I urge you to not pull away from her, no matter how uncomfortable you may feel. Even if your daughter begins to feel like a stranger to you, *she still needs you very much.*

- She needs you to tell her she's good enough.
- She needs you to tell her you see her.
- She needs you to tell her you're proud of her.
- She needs you to tell her she doesn't need a boy's approval to make her worthy.
- She needs you to hug her and kiss her on the cheek or forehead.
- She needs you to praise her great character traits.
- She needs you to tell her you think she's beautiful.
- She needs you to tell her you love seeing the woman she is becoming.

She has so many questions and insecurities in her life at this time about boys, friends, her body, and her abilities. Dads, you are God's method to help answer many of these questions from an emotionally engaged place. Moms do the same, but they're filling a different role in their daughters' lives. Dads, your role is unique and necessary. And for any teen girls who don't have a dad at home or one who is still living, other godly men can step into this critical role to provide reassurance, encouragement, courage, and security.

When I was in the fourth grade, I went in to say good night to my parents before bedtime, as I always did. I usually kissed my dad good night, but on this particular night, I proudly told him that maybe I was now too old to hug and kiss him good night. I said it and just left the room. I secretly wanted him to come after me, hug me, and tell me I would never be too old for his kisses.

That was the last time my dad kissed me—to this day. It's crazy that as I write this, in my late fifties, it still brings tears to my eyes. I wanted his appropriate affection. I wish he would have pursued me, but I didn't know how to tell him that. The truth was, he didn't have anyone else to tell him either. Dads, you don't have to go down this road. We're telling you now. It matters. Keep pursuing your daughter with patience, security, and affection that will make her feel safe, loved, and cherished.

After that conversation, my mom also stopped hugging and kissing me. I felt the loss of their affection so deeply that when my teen years arrived, I chose promiscuity to try to fill those needs. But it didn't; in fact, it only made it worse. Our kids are never too old to be hugged, kissed, or told that we love them very, very much. Keep doing it, even if it feels like you're hugging a cactus. Put on your big boy clothes and hug them anyway. After all, you can't take things personally during these years.

I never like to generalize and certainly very little is ever completely true for all people all the time. Yet what I'm about to share is something a lot of women (and not very many men) seem to understand: *women usually bond through communication*—which isn't always the case for the men in my life, as evidenced by what I call the "Golf Phenomenon." Dave can go golfing with a friend for five hours, and when he gets home, I can ask him what he and his friend talked about.

"Nothing," he'll lamely reply.

"What? You were gone for five hours, and you talked about nothing?"

"Well, I guess I did say, 'Nice shot!' a few times."

This is dumbfounding. With that kind of time on my hands, I'd know the name of my friend's second cousin's baby's favorite stuffed animal. Why? Because most women and girls tend to bond through communication. This doesn't mean guys can't bond through communication; they just tend to bond better when they're *doing* something together (golf excluded, apparently).

This explains how men go to war together, play on the same team together, or take an outdoor adventure together, only to feel a closeness that seems uncanny because they often haven't talked much during these experiences. They bond through shoulder-to-shoulder activity. Then oftentimes after the bonds forged during these activities are solidified, their conversations go really deep. I don't think women necessarily need any activity in order to foster good conversation. My point here is that dads may need to find something to do with their daughters before they will be comfortable talking with them on a mutually beneficial level.

My mom's brother was diagnosed with cancer when I was fifteen years old. My mom had to take him for chemotherapy treatments once a week and would usually be gone for the day. I was the youngest, and all of my siblings were either married or in college at the time. So Dad and I were left to fend for ourselves on those evenings.

Dad and I shared a great love for food and for eating out, so we'd head to Bill Knapp's, a local favorite in the little town of Findlay, Ohio. We would peruse the menu, talking about the food and what sounded good. I was generally in a rush to get back home to talk to my boyfriend or to get some homework done. Like all teens, I wasn't always enthusiastic about the time I had to spend with my parents.

The first time we went out for one of these dinners, I'll admit I was super nervous. I felt like I didn't really know my dad. He was much more attuned to my brothers, their sports, and their lives. My dad hadn't taken much of an interest in my sports, life, or activities. I felt like he didn't know me. Even so, here I was sitting across from someone with whom I thought the only thing we had in common was food.

Dinner was served and eaten, and I was ready to go. It just felt weird, and I knew he could tell I was antsy.

"You ready to go?" he asked with a half smile.

"Yep, I've got a lot to do," I sheepishly admitted.

"Well, I need another cup of coffee, and I really think we need a piece of that chocolate cake with a scoop of ice cream."

I rolled my eyes and groaned. I knew we'd be there another twenty minutes at least. He just smiled and motioned for the waiter to come over. We ordered, and then we ate the dessert and went home—me back to my busy teen life and him to his adult life.

But we kept needing to go out to dinner together. The more we did, the more those evenings with my dad became some of the sweetest nights of my life. My dad asks great questions.

He's a great talker, and he loves getting to know people. I could tell he was delighting in getting to know me, his youngest. He told me about his years growing up, and we laughed over these stories as another cup of coffee was poured. Then another. He asked me my opinion on things and eventually even asked for my advice on important matters.

Those dinners served as the starting point of a sweet relationship I still have with my dad. Yes, there were some issues of physical affection we didn't know how to navigate very well in those days, but all in all, my parents were the best models for Dave and me when it came to parenting teens. They were fun and not too controlling. They let us bend the rules sometimes, and, above all else, truly wanted to know us.

As I type this with tears streaming down my cheeks, I'm deeply grateful for my dad's pursuit of me. He'll be ninety-two years old by the time this book releases. He has stage 4 prostate cancer, along with a host of other medical conditions. Even so, he has been the model of how to make family a priority. He demands we all stay in contact with one another. He was also my mom's champion as he cared for her every single day for fifteen years during her battle with dementia.

My story about my dad is a great example of what can happen during the teen years if you'll just pursue instead of pulling away. Our relationship really didn't get started until that extra cup of coffee at Bill Knapp's.

Dad, it's never too late to pursue your little girl. She needs you!

Tip #2: Say Less, Pray More

When our kids entered the teen years, I found living out my faith to be very difficult. I had enjoyed their childhood and the process of being creative and teaching them the Bible, along with doing fun and meaningful devotionals with them before bedtime. But when they became teens, I saw them tuning me out, becoming bored, and just waiting for me to finish what I was saying. So most of the time I felt like I was failing. I was going to need to change my approach.

I decided to *say less and pray more*. Yes, it's a revolutionary idea for those of us who are big talkers and who love to teach life lessons with every butterfly, blue sky, and boo-booed knee. But for teens, I had to learn to say less and pray more, an idea that came from my good friend Kathy.

I began to pray with more attentiveness for my boys. I prayed for:

- small group leaders to join us in discipling them
- mission trips to change their perspectives
- friends to encourage them spiritually
- God's Word to come alive for them

And the list goes on. This time of praying also helped me start listening to God more than ever before. When I began to accept that my kids didn't need me in the same way as before, I started looking around me and looking at other ways God wanted to use me.

This led to a big discovery.

I realized our kids' friends needed nonjudgmental adults who would listen to them, pray for them, and offer advice when asked. These were some of my favorite days. I loved it when girls or guys would approach me and tell me about what they were facing. While my kids weren't as open to hearing me, these kids came to me in droves.

Don't feel threatened when your kids go to someone else for input. Instead, pray that they're going to people you can trust and who will encourage them in the same way—or even better than—you do. This is why community is so crucial. In the teen years, all of our friends befriended each other's kids. It was a sweet gift; otherwise they probably would have sought out the "infinite" wisdom of YouTube.

Remember, God loves your teens more than you do, so surrender them and stay (or get) busy learning to hear God's voice and obey it. *Talk less and pray more.* During these years, if the faith you hold dear sprouts in your teens, it will most definitely be *caught* more than *taught.* Try not to push it on them, or push them at all really.

FINAL THOUGHTS ON IDENTITY AND WORDS

I've struggled with identity for my entire life, which is a larger story for another time (or perhaps another book). Regardless, my own struggles have taught me that who you believe yourself to be is a critical variable that affects the way you'll approach everything else in life.

And when it comes to raising kids, you can multiply that variable by one hundred—which is why it is so crucial that you pay attention to the unique identities of your children, always guarding who God has made them to be. At times, you'll have to guard this precious identity from being tossed away by them. When they struggle, especially during the teen years, they will be the first ones to trash their own value and uniqueness as image bearers of God.

When the boys were younger, we would celebrate every birthday by eating dinner together. One of our traditions was to celebrate the birthday boy's life and birth by remembering and expressing all the great things about that person. Not only was it fun to hear siblings verbalize the talents and gifts of their brothers; it was transformational.

The older I get, the more aware I am that words of life are one of the greatest gifts we can bestow on others—especially our own family members. I wish I would have been more persistent in maintaining this tradition, but after hearing over and over how tired our kids were of this tradition and seeing them roll their eyes, I eventually caved in.

Even so, we still sometimes engage in a similar tradition at Thanksgiving, telling each person about the good we see in them and why we are grateful for them. It's especially sweet among grandkids, great-nieces, and great-nephews. Our words can be gifts that help shape and form, not their identities, but their beliefs and perceptions of their identities. Only God forms who they are, so our job is to never let them forget.

It's all too easy to see only the negatives, especially in our teens. We can become so afraid of *what our kids might do* that we forget *who our kids are.* I found myself doing a lot of critiquing, criticizing, and warning of our kids in their teen years. These days, I regret it. I was fearful they would do the wrong things, say the wrong things, drink the wrong things, date the wrong girls, and smoke the wrong things. I was so caught up in my fear of what the wrong things could do to them and how this could affect our reputation as their parents that I sometimes failed to call out what was still great in them. Sadly, I missed the opportunities to do so, which usually showed up disguised as their mistakes.

One spring night at the end of Cody's senior year, he walked into our room to say good night. He was the last one living at home. CJ was about to graduate from college. Austin was about to get married to his high school sweetheart, Kendall.

Cody would be setting off early for college in a month to play football. I was keenly aware that the days he'd be sleeping under our roof were limited.

He said good night as he hugged me. He was about to leave the room when I said, "Cody, wait a minute." He turned around, and our eyes met. "I just want you to know how proud I am of you and the man you have become. Look at you! You're going to college on a full ride, and you have worked your butt off to get that. You're such a great leader! I can't wait to see the impact you'll make on your team and at school. I'm not even sure you understand the power you carry and the influence you have to motivate and move people. It's actually pretty remarkable. You're amazing, and I know your life and walk with Jesus will be a light at Central Michigan. I can't wait to see what God does."

I can't exactly remember how Cody responded, but he thanked me quietly and went to his room. A few minutes later, he walked back into our room. Surprised, I turned around.

"Mom, I'm not the guy you think I am!" he emphatically said.

"You are totally that guy!" I said with passion. "I've seen it since you were little."

"No, you don't understand," he said, cutting me off. "I just got drunk last weekend for the first time. *That* is who I am, Mom!" Tears were rolling off his cheeks into his thin but growing beard.

Here was my chance. In the past, I would have gotten stuck on the "getting drunk" part, but I was beginning to realize what was more important. This wasn't about the drinking; this was about the identity.

"That's what you *did* last weekend; that's *not* who you are." I held him by the shoulders and looked squarely into his handsome face. "Do you hear me? Every word I said to you is true." We hugged and talked for a few more minutes, and off he went to bed.

I know what you're thinking. *Where were the consequences? The lectures? The life lessons?* You've read through most of the stages of parenting in detail, and there's definitely a lot of room for all that, but we were past those seasons. Besides, in the end I knew that as he was heading into his adult life, what he needed most was not more discipline, but rather the grace that reminded him of who God made him to be.

This may sound soft, but hear me out. As Romans 2:4 tells us, it is the *kindness* of God that leads us to repentance. That may not be popular parenting jargon, but I didn't write it. Think of it like this: When we intentionally reinforce our children's identities in Christ, we remind them of their truest selves, the ones that produce the behaviors that follow. Behavior follows identity, not the other way around. Behavior can also mask identity or draw someone away from it. When this is the threat—when a kid makes big mistakes—reminding them of their identity helps them to see how foreign it feels to be acting differently from who they know they really are.

Our minds, our patterns, and our enemy can all distract us from the things that matter most. As parents, we can get caught up in the bad choices our kids are making. That's what I did. The bigger question is, *Why are our kids making those decisions?* Satan is bombarding them with lies every day, and we need to be our kids' advocates, their compass that reorients them back to true north as we keep helping them discover who Christ says they are in him, and all of the unique gifts he has put inside them.

One day when the kids were older and home for the summer, all three boys were hanging out doing nothing.

I'm not one to loaf around much, so I often pointed them to the many chores and things they could be doing. As I was talking, I noticed they were all on their phones and laughing.

"What are you laughing about?" I asked, perturbed.

"We're all texting about you, Mom!" one of them laughingly said, just before they cracked up again.

I gave them a disgusted look, put on my walking shoes, and decided to blow off some steam and anger. I slammed the door harder than usual and began my six-mile trek. As I walked the first three miles, I prayed and complained about my kids and their lack of appreciation—and also about how wonderful I was as a mom. I made sure that God heard every detail of their disrespect and laziness.

Halfway through, I was so worked up that I actually challenged God: "Okay, you've heard what I think. I want to hear what *you* think about all this. I'm ready, God! Let's start with CJ."

"Isn't he such a delight?" I kid you not—that's what I heard.

"Ummm, no, he sure isn't a delight to me right now!" I fumed back.

For the next mile, I heard in my heart many of the reasons that God is so utterly enthralled with CJ, and even the pride he feels because he's such a unique human being. I felt confident it was God I was hearing because some of the things I heard were just not things I would ever say myself. At one point, I heard, "He's just like Nathanael, in whom I saw no deceit."

What? Who? I had to get my Bible out and reread the story of Jesus meeting Nathanael.[1] But the description was spot-on about CJ. He carries no pretense about anything and is a straight shooter.

1. See John 1:43–51.

God had now captured my attention, and I was ready to hear what he would say about Austin and Cody. With each of them, I felt like I was listening to an annoyingly proud daddy bragging about the greatness of his kids. I had never honestly asked God what he saw when he looked at our kids.

He told me I would be blown away by Austin when he became a father. Austin wasn't even married at that time. He went on and on about Austin and his talents, gifts, and passions.

The same rang true for Cody. He told me that Joshua was a fitting middle name because Cody would be a great leader like Joshua and others would follow him. Mind you, Cody was a young teen at the time, and I still didn't really know where he was spiritually.

"Cody?" I asked, a little dumbfounded.

God went on, bragging for about a mile on each child. After that walk, I've never looked at my sons in the same light. Earlier, I had been seeing them through earthly eyes, but after that walk, I saw them through heavenly eyes. Whether they would fully become all the things I heard that day didn't really matter. The world is a hard place to grow up, and the enemy is cunning. But I had a renewed sense of how to see them, how to pray for them, and what to say to them that would help them remember who they were made to be.

Moms and dads, you have *way* more power than you realize. It's never too late to start speaking words of life into your kids that reinforce what God thinks about them.

— Reflections —

FIRST SON: CJ

- Giving me freedom and loosening the rules as I became older helped me to really appreciate you guys as parents, even when I was still a teen.
- I can't speak for Cody, but the little amount of drinking I did during my junior year stopped during my senior year. I felt like it wasn't fair to you guys to drink when you were being reasonable, extending my curfew, and not giving me stupid, irrational rules to follow, like some of my friends' parents were giving them.
- I really liked that you guys would stay up until midnight and talk to my friends when we were hanging out at our house together.
- I think I learned how to have long conversations with girls by listening to Mom talk to the girls in my friend group in middle school and high school.
- I probably would have become an atheist if you had shut down my questioning of things like Young Earth creationism when I was in high school and college.

CHAPTER 11

MY TOP FIVE *Parenting Mistakes*

Friendship Stage, Ages Eighteen Plus

Brace yourself! Everything you've been working toward with little kids and bigger kids will suddenly change—and you'll find yourself staring into the eyes of adults instead of children. This is the stage the Wilsons are in now and we're still learning all about it. Relationships do not stop at the age of eighteen, so there's always hope for ongoing connection.

We've had to be honest about where we didn't get it right as parents when our sons were younger. Yes, this can hurt, but it's also a necessary part of becoming healthy together in the friendship stage. We're not saying you have to sit down and talk through every single miscue of their lives. We're pointing to more of an attitude issue. It's about a humbling of the heart and mind that allows you to acknowledge your lack of perfection as a parent. Believe it or not, as our children become parents themselves, their empathy for your plight as their parents will increase exponentially—and that's a beautiful moment.

One of the many conflicts that Ann and I (Dave) had in the

first ten years of our marriage when our boys were young was that she felt I was often too harsh and critical with my words. She tried to point out that I often came off as a know-it-all and that it made her and the kids feel stupid. She said I would roll my eyes at her, scoff, and walk away when I was frustrated, which caused her to shut down and pull away.

When she would address my harshness, I just couldn't see it at all. I'd get mad at her for being critical of me, which usually led to me yelling at her, even calling her crazy as I rolled my eyes. I had no clue that I was doing the very thing she was upset with me about. I was convinced she was exaggerating just to get my attention and make me feel bad. And I was certain that I never did any of that with our kids.

I was oblivious.

All that changed when we made a weekend visit to her parents in Ohio. Our boys were right around the toddler stage, and I had pulled out the video camera and was filming us playing in the family room. This was before iPhone cameras, and I had the camera mounted on a tripod, filming us rolling around on the floor. Later that day, we popped the video into the VHS player and showed it to Ann's parents.

As we watched, I noticed that several times I rolled my eyes at something Ann or the boys said or did. But it got worse. When the fun and games came to an end, I realized I had never turned off the record function, so it kept taping after we were done playing. That's when it happened right there for all of us to see: a recorded fight between Ann and me.

The video captured it in living color. Ann said, "You did it again. You were harsh with me and the boys, and you even rolled your eyes like we're a bunch of idiots!"

I yelled back, "You're crazy! You're just making stuff up—and let me tell you what else . . ." By that point, I had jumped up to hit the stop button. I looked over at my in-laws, and their faces were stone-cold. My father-in-law had a look that said, *Busted.* I looked over at Ann, and she was smiling from ear to ear. I heard her whisper, "Thank you, Jesus."

Busted was right. I couldn't believe my own eyes. I was a jerk, and I hadn't known it. Everything that Ann had been trying to tell me was right there in front of me for the whole world to see. I needed to change, and I needed to change *right then.*

The truth is, we make many mistakes as parents. We made more than our fair share, and so will you. One of the best ways to avoid making certain mistakes is to learn from others' mistakes. So we thought it could be helpful to share some of our mistakes after thirty-four years of being parents and now grandparents. We could give you hundreds of examples, but we limit these to our top five.

MISTAKE #1: I LEFT MY SOUL AT THE OFFICE

One of the things I struggled with as a dad was being fully present in my home. I'd bring all my energy and focus to my job, but often when I came home, my soul was still at work. I remember stepping into the house one time after work when five-year-old Austin yelled, "Mommy, Daddy's home!"

"No he's not," Ann replied.

Austin looked super confused, as did I. He said, "Look, Mommy, he's standing right here!"

"I know he's standing there, honey, but he's actually still at the office."

She was right. I was physically in our home, but my heart was still back at the office as I dealt with work problems in my head. It was much easier to bring more energy to my work than

I did to my home. I would come home exhausted and be resentful if Ann asked me to help her. My thoughts were so selfish. *Do you have any idea how hard my day has been? I just need a break!* Of course, Ann was thinking the exact same thing—and truth be told, her day with two toddlers and a nursing baby was truthfully more draining than mine. Of course, I didn't understand this, until I had to take care of those three for an entire day (yes, just one day) by myself. I couldn't even function by day's end.

A truth hit me in those early parenting years that changed my perspective: *My job as a dad* is the most important job I have. It is more important than my work. As a pastor, I am a shepherd to thousands of people, but they are not my legacy. I may stand before Jesus one day and be held accountable for the people of my church in some ways, but not in the way I will be held accountable as a parent. I desperately needed to change my perspective and bring more energy to my home.

To help with this, I developed a ritual on my way home from work. As I turned into our subdivision, I'd slow down and look at the first mailbox on our street. In my mind, I opened that mailbox and made an exchange. I dropped off my work role and picked up my husband/dad role. As I pulled into our driveway, I would pray a little prayer: "Jesus, give me the strength to bring all I've got to this most important job of loving and serving Ann and my boys. Help me to be the husband and dad you have called me to be." *Okay, let's do this!*

I would seek to bring everything I had to my most important job. I failed many times, but my daily ritual helped me at least try to improve on getting my priorities in the proper order.

The other area in which I wasn't always fully present had to do with sharing my heart with my sons. I didn't realize this until my adult sons pointed it out. As I shared earlier, I often gave my soul to our congregation and kept it from my boys. This was a big failure. I shared intimate and raw details of my heart in a sermon with thousands of people from the stage yet failed to share these same struggles with my sons. They would learn more about their dad in my sermon than they did in our family room. This communicated that the people in our church are more important than the people who bear my last name.

This came up recently when Cody and I were preaching together at our church. For the past three years, Cody has been my co-pastor, and it has been a complete joy to serve alongside him. When Cody signed with the Detroit Lions as a receiver out of college, I thought being the chaplain and having my son on the team would be the ultimate utopia. It was incredible to watch him occupy a locker beside Calvin Johnson, but it has been even more amazing to do ministry together.

Every once in a while, we've partnered on the sermon together. We sit on stools onstage and go back and forth with various notes. We preached recently on mental health, and I had told Cody to be as honest as he wanted to be about our relationship in this message. At one point, Cody commented on a story I've told many times about a "rite of passage" trip he and I took when he was thirteen years old. I've shared this story at church and around the country as an example of how to lead one's son into manhood.

The gist of the story is that the trip opened up conversation with Cody on several important topics. I wrote down a list of topics on a sheet of paper and handed it to him as we began our six-hour drive. I said, "We're going to talk about each of these topics in whatever order you want. So just pick a topic, and let's start talking about it."

Cody looked at the sheet and said, "Uh, we're going to talk about women's breasts?"

"Yep."

"Okay, and we're going to talk about masturbation?"

"Yep." Needless to say, many intimate topics made its way onto that sheet, as well as some less sensational but equally important ones like competition, integrity, and so forth.

I have shared from the stage many times that this trip was incredible for both of us and how important it is as a dad to talk about these kinds of things with your kids. Well, that day in our sermon, Cody said, "I have to be honest that it wasn't as great of a trip for me as it was for Dad."

I had never heard him say this before, especially in front of thousands of people. I looked over and asked, "What does that mean?"

"Dad, I don't want to hurt you, but it's really awkward when your dad suddenly wants to talk about intimate things with you when he has never talked intimately with you about anything before this moment." I could tell that as he said it, those feelings had been buried in him for years. And at that very moment, I knew he was right.

And I knew it probably wasn't only Cody who felt that way. Ann and my other sons have shared similar feelings. If there's one thing I would request a do-over for as a husband and dad, it would be to bring my heart home to my family and let them in. That's a really scary thing to do—and believe it or not, it can be easier to do it with complete strangers. But your family deserves to have all of you. Don't make the same mistake I made. Open up your heart to the most important people in your life today. I know it can be hard, scary, and awkward, but you may never get this moment again with your son or daughter. Seize it while you can.

MISTAKE #2: I WAS NICER TO THE MAILMAN THAN TO MY KIDS

Have you ever been caught yelling at your family when the doorbell rang? You've got spit flying out of your mouth as you scream something at your kids, and then you get to the front door, open it with a calm smile on your face, and say, "Hello, what can I do for you?" Complete strangers often get a better version of us than our families get, which makes us seem like strangers to our families.

I tended to be happy with others but intense with my kids. I was constantly trying to build something great into our boys, and I was always concerned whether they were responding the way I wanted. Every little misstep they made became a mammoth teaching point.

I should have enjoyed life with them more. Ann brought this attitude of "make a memory" to our home. She was as intense as any mom could be, but at the same time, she brought a contagious joy to everyone most of the time. I was almost always thinking about how much money we were spending or how we were being perceived by others rather than just letting loose and enjoying the moment—or in Ann's words, "making this moment memorable." I absolutely love the joy that Ann brought to our home; in fact, I envy it.

One summer day, I was standing in our kitchen when I noticed CJ's car rolling slowly down our basketball court toward the woods. This was the first car he had bought with the lawnmowing money he had saved for years. I noticed there was no one in the car, which was picking up speed as it rolled down our sloped court. I immediately sprinted out the back door to try to stop the car before it entered the woods. Our court has a pretty good slope, so the car was picking up more steam than I was.

Just as I got to the car, it slammed into a tree behind our court. The front bumper was somewhat dented, but the damage was minimal. Immediately, I began yelling, "How did this happen? Who released the parking brake on CJ's car? Everyone get out here *now*!" I was pretty steamed. The real reason I was angry was that this was going to cost me a few dollars.

After interrogating all three boys in the backyard, it became apparent that eleven-year-old Cody had gotten into the car alone, pushed down the parking brake, and shifted the car into neutral. He then got out of the car, not realizing what he had done. Obviously those actions led the car to repark itself in the woods. As I stood there looking at the wreckage, I blew a gasket.

I was screaming loud enough for the entire neighborhood to hear. Then Ann came walking out of the door laughing. She had watched me sprint out of the house to try to catch the car, and now was watching me lose it. She just couldn't contain her laughter. I mean, she was belly laughing so hard that I screamed, "You think this is funny? Are you kidding me? Do you know how much this is going to cost?" And she just flopped down on the grass and held her sides as she laughed hysterically. The next thing I knew, the boys started laughing with her. They all just looked at me and kept laughing and laughing.

Ann's joy was contagious to everyone but me. I just couldn't see what they thought was so funny. And then it hit me. For a second, in my mind's eye I could see what Ann had seen—namely, her husband sprinting through the kitchen, out the back door, and across the deck, all the while trying to stop a car that was not going to be caught, no matter how fast I ran. And then this husband began ranting and screaming about a dent in a bumper that could be fixed in no time for very little money.

Then I started laughing too. I couldn't help myself.

Listen, younger Dave (and any mom or dad reading this right now): it's time to loosen up and enjoy the moments God gives you, no matter how intense they may feel at the time. I almost missed this invitation to joy because I was just too uptight. Every day of parenting will have moments when God is offering us joy—and usually in the middle of chaos. These are moments to step back and capture this situation as a memory.

But hear me when I say that *we have to choose it*; it will not choose us. And if we don't choose it, we will miss it—and it will be gone forever.

MISTAKE #3: I FORGOT THE BULL'S-EYE

We have written much about the target that we are shooting at as we raise our children. Ann and I had written down our mission of raising L3 warriors, and we talked about it often. And yet we often got caught up in striving for values and priorities that, in the end, simply weren't that important.

It's so easy for us parents to lose our focus in little increments. It may not be a conscious thing, but distractions creep in until our focus has migrated to wanting our kids to be successful or happy. We lose focus on our true bull's-eye, even though we've already agreed that it matters so much more than these worldly values.

Have you ever heard this one from parents: "Man, I just want to give them a better life than I had." There's nothing necessarily wrong with this goal, but if it becomes our sole focus, it'll be the wrong focus. The right focus is this: *wanting to develop a young man or woman of character.* We should aim to raise adults who walk in integrity, who are honest, who are willing to work hard, and who live for things that are eternal.

These are the things that produce real men and women who can be trusted.

This journey is not just about their happiness, popularity, or success. Trust me, if you're helping your kids advance only in athletics, the temptations to chase these things will be very real. All of these things matter to everyone else, but they do not last. It's easy to lose focus and find yourself living—and helping your kids live—for the same things.

Remember the fence we try to build for our kids? When the bull's-eye begins to shift (sorry to mix metaphors, but you should be able to follow this), we end up moving the fence because we want our kids to be happy. If they're going to be mad because we won't let them go to a certain party, we're tempted to think, *Do I really want them to be mad at me over a silly party?* But deep inside, we know that something about this party just isn't right. But sometimes we want them to be our friends so much that we miss the goal of developing character, and we move the boundary.

There's a time to pick our battles—and there's a time to insist on the bull's-eye. We must remember that adversity builds character. Tough times, hard work, and difficulty—the right kinds for where they are in their lives—create resistance, but it makes our children stronger. Rarely does character get developed in easy times; it gets developed in tough times. Tough times build tough people. In fact, you could make a good case that the Detroit Lions have the most character of any team in the NFL!

Character isn't built by giving our kids everything they want; it's built by exercising maturity and wisdom to adopt the best strategies to help develop them into men and women of tried and tested character. I guarantee you that my single mom never wrote down a bull's-eye for raising me as her son, but she had purpose. She wanted me to be a man of character. A man of integrity. A hardworking man who could be trusted. And boy did she make me work! I often hated it. Like when I had to mow the yard. Or resurface the driveway. I also painted the house and shoveled the driveway each winter.

Mom also didn't have much money, so I had to buy anything and everything I wanted. (Wonder where I get my issues with not wanting to spend money?) I was in a band, and I bought my own guitar. I bought my amps. I bought everything. At the time, I hated all of it. I would yell at Mom and say, "All my friends' parents buy their guitars! Why do I have to buy my own?"

Mom would say, "Yep, go mow another yard. Go shovel another driveway. Go make some money, and you can get that guitar." And guess what? I appreciate that guitar. I still have my first guitar. It's hanging on the wall in my office. As I look back, I realize my mom really understood the target at which she was shooting—and it wasn't the same target everybody else was aiming at.

We're aiming at a target called character. And hard work is a good way to help get there.

MISTAKE #4: I NEGLECTED MY MARRIAGE

Another of my many mistakes is that I put so much emphasis on raising our kids that I sometimes neglected our marriage. It's easy to do. Raising children feels like it takes every ounce of energy we have, so we have little left to pour into our marriage. We all know that our children are blessings straight from God, but they are not the center of the universe. I know it may be hard to hear this, but your spouse should come before your kids.

I get it. We can become disappointed in our spouse and marriage during these years. Our spouse may seem to not be loving us like we dreamed they would, which makes our marriage feel flat. So what do we do to keep going? We pour our heart and soul into our kids instead, not dealing with the issues in our marriage. Obviously it is a good thing to pour your life into your kids, but when it causes one's marriage to suffer, it becomes a bad thing.

One of the best things we can do for our kids is to love our spouse well. A great marriage brings security to the home and makes our kids feel safe. When a husband and wife do the hard work to keep their marriage strong, their marriage creates an atmosphere that fills the home. You can walk in that home and smell the sweet aroma. You can see the security on the faces of the little ones who live there safely under the shelter of their parents' marriage. It is one of the greatest gifts you can give your kids, but it is super hard work. It doesn't just happen. Great marriages pay a high price to stay great.

On our very first visit to the pediatrician after our first son was born, the doctor asked us if we had our first date night scheduled. Ann and I looked at each other. *Date night? Are you crazy? We're not leaving this little guy for anything.* The doctor taught us very early how important it was to get away and work on this vitally important relationship. We've been dating ever since. And guess who dates now that they have kids? Our adult children have copied what they saw us do. Of course, we try to make it easy for them, since we beg to watch our grandkids when they go out!

We mentioned in our book *Vertical Marriage* an important rhythm to grow your marriage both vertically (in relationship with God) and horizontally (in relationship with each other) at the same time. It involves something that's built into our calendar each day, each week, and each year. Use the letters PD, DW, RA as a reminder to Pray Daily, Date Weekly, and Retreat Annually.

Check out these principles and practices, but above all, keep your marriage a healthy priority in your home. It will sustain you as a parent.

MISTAKE #5: I DIDN'T HUG ENOUGH

I'm not a very affectionate or touchy-feely person. It bugs me if someone comes up and gives me a long hug, so I don't hug others very often either. The bottom line, though, is that this is a bunch of baloney when it comes to our kids. Kids long to be loved and hugged by their parents. They may say it isn't true—and I said the same thing when I was a kid. But as we learned from Ann's story about no longer giving good night hugs and kisses, deep down *we all* want to be loved and shown affection. An appropriate, meaningful touch communicates love.

When my boys were young, I hugged them and kissed them all the time. I lay in bed with them at night to talk and laugh. But as they got older and became men, I stopped doing these things. Because doing so felt awkward, I pulled away from being affectionate with them.

Big mistake.

Hug your kids at any and every age. It doesn't matter whether or not you're an affectionate person. Get over your fear and do it. In fact, put down this book and go do it right now, if you still can. Otherwise, do it the next time you see them.

They will be glad you did, and you will too.

— Reflections —

THIRD SON: CODY

- My dad is my best friend. He has been a father, a coach, a mentor, and a ministry partner. One of the greatest joys of my life was being able to pastor together at his church. I am so grateful for him and the new legacy he has helped carve in our family through the power of Jesus.
- My dad is one of the most courageous people I know to be able to write his faults in a book for the world to see. He is still striving to be a great dad and is putting in the work to become more emotionally present. I'm grateful for that and believe the best is yet to come in our family.
- Despite what my dad said in this chapter, he is a very kind, loving, and fun person. I am grateful to be the son of a dad who basically never belittled me or spoke down to me.
- Regarding the story about Dad and me preaching together on mental health, a few corrections. Dad brought up the dynamics of our relationship spontaneously; it wasn't in our notes. As a matter of fact, the last time we had talked about the dynamics of our relationship was four months earlier, which had left me crying in his kitchen over deep-rooted pain from his emotional absence. There had been very little to no follow-up on this conversation until out of nowhere, Dad brought it up *spontaneously on the stage*.
- I think Dad finds it easier to share his life as he looks at thousands of heads rather than when he looks deep into one pair of eyes. It's a monologue rather than a dialogue—a form of intimacy that's not quite as deep.
- I find that sometimes trying harder doesn't equate to connecting deeper. Our hard work can at times pull us away from loving and connecting deeply with others.

- As a parent, I'm working on my ability to *just be*. Be present. Be in the moment. Be aware of my wife and sons' needs and emotions.
- At times, I just needed my dad to sit down with me, look me in the eyes, and ask, "How are you?" When I messed up in high school, I needed my dad to be present and speak into my life with love and wisdom. I needed him to know the names of the girls I dated. I needed him to be able to go out to eat with me and ask questions without it being awkward. It's not your kid's responsibility to drive the conversation. Ask them questions, and don't put the pressure on them to ask you the right questions.
- Rites of passages are great, but in my opinion, daily and weekly connections with your kids are more important.
- Your kids need to know that family is more important than work. Your calendar and lifestyle should communicate this more than your words. If you're never home, ask yourself why. What are you running from?
- I believe my dad is a hugging person. He just doesn't know it yet. He shut down his emotions in order to survive his upbringing. Don't make the truth of who you had to become in a season of survival overshadow the truth of who God truly created you to be. I had to realize that my dad's inability to connect emotionally had more to do with a trauma-filled upbringing than with something that was wrong with me.
- The truth is, the wounds of your past will spill out onto your kids if you're not careful. Deep wounds sometimes need professional help, rehab, and time to heal. Take the time to heal. It has the potential to change everything about your life and legacy. If you never heal from your past, you will always have a painful future. As a parent, you're worth taking the necessary time to be healed internally. Remember that changing a legacy starts with allowing Jesus to change you.

CHAPTER 12

EMBRACING THE *Journey Ahead*

As we come to the end of our time together, we remind you that our content is incomplete. This is exactly what it feels like to be a parent—the job is never done, the changes never stop coming, and the stories never end. This can seem overwhelming, but it's also the reason there is so much hope—the future is still out there, no matter where you've been in your past. Let us remind you of a few things about this future.

I (Ann) talked a lot about making memories as my mantra, and I hope you can see how this is still a huge value in our family. The memories, some good and some not so good, are still with us. And we continue to make new ones.

However, the other concept I wanted to build into our home was for our kids to see the beauty that comes from a close and personal relationship with Jesus. As you grapple with what this means for you, let me encourage you in some practical ways.

When we first had kids, I realized quickly that finding quiet time with Jesus seemed nearly impossible. My sister was a morning person, so she set her alarm for 5:00 a.m. every day to be able to have her time alone with Jesus. It's important to figure this out and to find what works best for you.

I told myself I was a night person. I wasn't, but I told myself I was, even as I fought the guilt that came because I wasn't waking up before the sun like all of the "spiritual" people. Each night, I fell into bed exhausted and depleted—and I opened my Bible, only to fall asleep after reading a couple of verses or getting halfway through my prayer.

Maybe you've been there.

I just didn't know how people could find time to pray and read the Bible. Some of you have figured it out, and I applaud you. I had to get work done and laundry done, and when the boys were little, I'd use their naptimes to accomplish these tasks.

After the kids were out of the home, I went back to work full-time. Maybe that's your reality with young kids. I feel you—when I would come home after many hours of work, I felt equally depleted. If you are a full-time working mom or dad, you carry a heavy load, and you deserve an all-inclusive trip to somewhere tropical—with an attendant bringing you food and drinks for at least a month.

So with all of this going on, how do we grow deeper in our walk with Jesus?

I'll share what worked for me, hoping it may give you some ideas. Of course, it changed with the varying seasons. But for me, when the kids were young, I simply began praying all throughout the day. When I was doing dishes or cleaning up in the kitchen, I prayed simple prayers, maybe a sentence or two. Washing dishes reminded me to confess my sin and ask God to cleanse and help me. When I did the laundry, I got in a habit of praying for the person whose clothes I was folding. When we got in the car and buckled the kids into their car seats, I prayed out loud, thanking God for another day, along with bringing to him the array of other things on my mind.

This lasted all the way through high school and beyond. I still do it by myself.

We prayed out loud before meals; we prayed for ouchies, for friends, and for family. Before bed, we read books about God that were appropriate for their age. We had prayer requests at bedtime and prayed for those things before falling asleep. We had a children's Bible we went through.

Why am I telling you this right now? Because I was always amazed at how God used those Bible and devotional times as food for *my* hungry soul.

Deuteronomy 6 began to be lived out in our home without us even realizing it. Unknowingly, I wasn't just having a "devotional time"; I was experiencing a "devotional life."

> Hear, O Israel: The LORD our God, the LORD is one. Love the LORD your God with all your heart and with all your soul and with all your strength. These commandments that I give you today are to be on your hearts. Impress them on your children. Talk about them when you sit at home and when you walk along the road, when you lie down and when you get up.
>
> *Deuteronomy 6:4–7*

Our faith isn't just "an hour on Sunday morning" thing. Our faith is about our relationship with the God of the universe who loves us and died for us so we could be in relationship with him. God wants to know us, talk to us, encourage us, be there for us, and reveal himself to us. So don't get caught up in thinking your walk with God needs to fit into a certain box (or that you're not spiritual if it doesn't). Just learn to feed your soul and be in connection with God all day long. At work. At home. In the car. In the shower. When possible, do it out loud and on purpose for your kids to see. Confess your sin in front of them. Talk to God in front of them, and let them see your joy, tears, frustrations, awe, and reverence to our Father—because he is also *their* Father.

You may not feel like doing it, but that doesn't make you a fake if you do it out of belief, trusting even when you don't see or feel. That's just *faith*. On the other hand, don't do it just so they can see you do it. That's just *fake*. Make sure it's authentic. Kids can sniff out fakes. Let it become such a way of life that your kids won't even realize until they leave home that this isn't the way everyone lives.

Cody went on a mission trip during his sophomore year of college. As he told us the details of the trip, we could see that his faith had taken on a whole new dimension. He was on fire for Jesus! He said it was cool to be with other kids who had not grown up in a Christ-following home. He said they prayed as a group about everything they were doing on the mission trip. Cody said they saw an ambulance go by, and one of the leaders quickly prayed out loud for the person that ambulance was on the way to help. A young woman also mentioned how great it was to pray about both big and small things throughout the day.

Cody looked at me and said, "Mom, I realized I had seen you do that throughout my entire life and that I took it for granted. Thanks for showing me that."

Tears fill my eyes as I type these words because as parents, we have no guarantees and sometimes no awareness that anything really got through to them or stuck there. Some of us will never know. Some of us think it's too late because our kids are too old to glean any spiritual knowledge from us.

Cody reminded me that God can use the completely inadequate seeds that were planted to produce more in their hearts than we could ever imagine.

My ninety-one-year-old dad didn't go to church when we were growing up. Honestly, he never has. However, he has always been a great advocate for me and Dave, believing in who we are and what we do. He simply hasn't ever talked much about faith—and over the years, I may have pushed him too hard at times on the subject.

My mom—his wife of almost seventy years—died a short time ago. My dad was in the hospital with pneumonia at the time. It was tragic because he couldn't be with her in her last days. He was heartbroken to lose his sweetheart and the love of his life. He wasn't present with her when she slipped into the arms of Jesus. When my brother went to the hospital to tell my dad that Mom had passed in the middle of the night, my dad was fully alert.

He sat up and told my brother, "I know she's gone. Jesus was just here and told me she was with him and that she was dancing in heaven." My dad then prayed the most beautiful prayer of thanks to God for my mom, their life together, and our family. He gave God all the glory and credit for his family.

My brother said he and his wife, Jenny, and my other sister-in-law, Kathy, all stood there with their mouths wide open. You see, none of us had ever heard my dad pray in our entire lives. We thought he had faith, but he was never one to talk about it. Hearing this story was one of the greatest gifts given to us during the dark days of losing my best friend, my mom. You see, it's never too late to inspire your kids. It's never too late to pray for them. It's never too late to go to God for your prodigal—no matter how old they are. Don't give up hope!

If you've never done anything like this before with your kids, just be honest with them. Kids respond to it because real honesty always works best, and Jesus was the most real and honest person on the planet. Just tell them how you feel. Say, "I want God to be more of a part of my life. I'm trying to grow in my faith, so you may hear me talking about him more or praying out loud more—and praying for you more. It may feel weird or awkward at first, but I want him to be a big part of my life and our home. Will you help me learn here?"

Again, there's no need to act holier-than-thou. Take it from someone who is holier-than-none—this is a surefire way to shut down the faith conversation before it ever gets started. Be real. Be open. Be humble.

If your spouse isn't on the same page or if you're in a blended family and your ex is on a different page, that's okay too. No, this is not a perfect situation, but God's grace covers a multitude of missed targets. You do you in humility and community, and let God work on the issues of your past and the hearts of others in your life. I'm not saying this is easy. I'm just telling you that you won't fully know what God is up to until later, sometimes years later. No matter what you see now, don't lose hope; rather, keep seeking an authentic faith.

If you're serving as foster parents, this could be the greatest gift you give your kids as they live under your roof, even if it's only for a short time. We've watched Austin and Kendall do this with their foster kids. Make a memory with them while you can. Plant love and peace into little hearts that may have seen more than their share of hurt and turbulence. You can't control the eternal outcomes—or even the earthly ones. But you can keep waking up and choosing to trust and grow again today, even if you blew it yesterday.

BACK TO LEGACY AND THE TARGET

A few final thoughts as you seek to continue a godly legacy or change a godless legacy. We believe you will need these three elements:

- power of God
- people of God
- practice

Power of God

Remember that we truly have no chance to create anything significant or lasting by our own strength. We need God's supernatural power. Cody recently preached on God's power by using his cell phone as an example. Our cell phones do not work when the battery is dead. They have to be charged, and they can't be charged by just any charger. Apple makes a lightning charger that fits perfectly with an iPhone.

People are exactly the same. We can't function without power. We are designed by our Creator to find real power only in a real, messy, grace-filled, fully devoted life with him. God made us to find life and power only when fueled by his supernatural power. The other chargers of this world that promise to fulfill us simply don't fit and don't work. They can even catch us on fire—in a bad way.

Raising kids is absolutely exhausting and frustrating. Without God's strength, we will fail daily, and even with his power, we will still fail daily. However, he is gracious to remind us that our failures are not final. When God is invited into our homes, he brings redemption for our mistakes, especially when we choose to live real lives in front of our kids. We want our kids to have soft, quick-to-repent hearts. Well, guess what?

Our own failures give us the prime opportunity to show them who we really are in Christ, to confess and make it right—the very thing we want them to do as well.

You may have taken six months to read this book because you have a two-year-old hanging on your legs and rubbing snot on your pants. We've been there. It can push you to your wit's end. You may not feel like it, but you are so very loved, and God's power is available for these frustrating moments of exhaustion.

You don't have to be a perfect parent to be loved perfectly by God.

When I (Dave) first showed a verse to nine-year-old CJ from the Ten Commandments about God punishing the children for the sins of the parents down to the third and fourth generation, his response was classic: "Dad, don't sin!"

The truth is, none of us have the power in ourselves to not sin. This isn't just jargon; it's Scripture. Romans 7:18 (ESV) reads, "For I know that nothing good dwells in me, that is, in my flesh. For I have the desire to do what is right, but not the ability to carry it out." Trust me, we've tried, and we bet you have too. We can resist temptation for a day or two, but not for the long term. We need God's Holy Spirit living in us and empowering us, or else we will pass along a legacy of sin and addiction to our kids.

I (Dave) will never forget the day I discovered porn on our home computer. First of all, we should have known better than to place our home computer in the basement. That was just stupid. Your computer should be in the center of traffic so it's always in the sight of Mom and Dad. I showed Ann what I had found in our computer history, which is why you should be checking your history regularly if you have kids older than six. Of course, Ann's first question was whether this porn viewing was done by me. It was a valid question because she knew I had struggled with porn in the past. I had been very honest with her about my issues, but this was not my browsing history.

We had an idea which son it was based on age, so we asked him, and he admitted that this porn history was his. I had always wondered what my reaction would be the day I found one of our sons struggling with porn. I figured I'd be angry and want to scold him. Or perhaps I would pretend that I didn't know what had happened so I wouldn't have to confess my own sin in this area. Yet here we sat with our own son, who was sitting in the same situation I had sat in so many times.

I wept.

I found myself weeping because I know the struggle. I told my thirteen-year-old son about my struggle with porn and how the initial cracking open of this door can lead to a lifetime of sexual temptation. I was so sad in that moment because I had hoped he and all my sons would make it through life without this struggle. And yet there we were.

I vowed to him that day to help him walk this journey together. Men need other men in their lives to win this battle. We cannot win this one alone, and we can't do it without the supernatural power of God. If we try to win this battle or any other struggle with sin under our own strength, we will consistently fall and be enslaved to pride, fear, and lies. That will be the legacy we pass on.

I (Ann) reminded both Dave and our son of the amazing truth that the resurrection power that raised Jesus from the dead lives in us. If we have chosen to answer God's call to us to surrender our lives, we don't have to walk around as weak, powerless humans. We truly can live a powerful life—a life that is impossible to live without him.

We love *The Incredibles* movies. Each member of the Incredibles family has a supernatural power that enables them to do things no human can do. They are called "Supers" because they have superpowers. The truth is, you and I could be called "Supers" too because we have the literal *power of God* within us. Our lives will look drastically different than they did before. God's power is the legacy we can pass on, even in our weakness—because even then, he is supremely strong.

People of God

We simply cannot raise a family alone. We need other godly people alongside us to help us raise the children God has entrusted to us. One of God's greatest blessings to us has been our group of friends who have helped us raise our sons, but those friendships didn't just happen. We pursued them and they pursued us, and as a result, our community has walked together for more than twenty-five years.

We have helped each other through mountaintop highs and some extremely low valleys. We have celebrated together at our kids' weddings, graduations, scholarships, and vacations. We have also cried and struggled with our kids as a group through divorce, addictions, and broken hearts. We were not created to go through any of these things alone. Together, our joys are doubled, and our grief is cut in half.

One day, our friend Rob stopped by to give us a heads-up. He said he had pulled into our subdivision and noticed a car with a young teen driver. The kid was driving recklessly, which was very dangerous, given that little children were playing in their front yards. As Rob got closer to the car to see what idiot would be driving so carelessly, he discovered that it was our youngest son, Cody, who was sixteen at the time. Rob cut him off and forced him to stop. He confronted him and told him how dangerous his driving was.

That's what brothers and sisters in Christ do for one

another to help us raise our kids and create a legacy that honors Jesus. Rob could have waited for one of us to come out and stop Cody from driving dangerously, but that would have endangered both Cody and other kids. He knew he had our blessing to help us within the boundaries we all share in Christ. The thing is, many a believer would be super offended by someone really living in true community such as this—this is a part of our fence, and while it can get messy, we know we need people. It's not always easy, but it is desperately needed.

A few weeks later, Rob and I (Dave) were sitting in a high school gym watching Rob and Michelle's daughter play basketball. The game was close, and the referees were doing their best to control the game. Rob started railing on the refs loudly from the stands. He was out of control and causing quite a stir. At one point, I thought the refs were going to throw him out of the gym.

As I watched him, I realized he had no idea how ridiculous he looked. After the game, I confronted Rob and told him that his behavior embarrassed his wife and his daughter. I said it gently but firmly, as only a good friend could. He immediately recognized that his behavior dishonored his family and was a bad witness for Jesus. He thanked me for pointing this out and changed his behavior in the future. I sat at many more athletic contests with him over the years, and he truly honored Christ and his family from then on.

This sort of thing should be normal for believers who are living in real community. We aren't saying you should walk up to total strangers and confront them about their sin. These kinds of corrections come out of deep relationships built over years of trust, as well as a willingness to be sharpened by one another to become more like Jesus. If you're a believer and this kind of thing seems outlandish to you, let us humbly say that your life is lacking something for which there is no biblical substitute. Community is that important. We all struggle here, but never giving up on these kinds of relationships is the right kind of struggle.

Yes, we share these stories of correction, but it is just as much about sharing encouragement, joy, experiences, knowledge—just sharing life. I (Ann) live life with two other moms who pray and fast together every Wednesday for all of our kids. What a comfort to know that I don't have to do all the praying alone. I can be weak. Human. Hurting. Yet I can know that my family is still being guarded and supported.

The life-changing *power* of God leads us to live life with the *people* of God.

Practice

One of our favorite Bible passages that applies to the family is found at the end of a long sermon. (People say Dave's sermons are long at thirty minutes, but this one took a couple of days!) Jesus preached it on a hill near the Sea of Galilee. It's known as the Sermon on the Mount, and Jesus brought it to an end with these words:

> "Therefore everyone who hears these words of mine and puts them into practice is like a wise man who built his house on the rock. The rain came down, the streams rose, and the winds blew and beat against that house; yet it did not fall, because it had its foundation on the rock. But everyone who hears these words of mine and does not put them into practice is like a foolish man who built his house on sand. The rain came down, the streams rose, and the winds blew and beat against that house, and it fell with a great crash."
>
> *Matthew 7:24–27*

This passage shows us one of the most important truths about raising a family that is focused on the vertical. We can go to church all we want. We can quote and memorize Scripture all we want. But if we don't put it into *practice* in our normal, daily lives, it's all just a waste of time.

The difference in the two houses wasn't whether they *knew* the words of Jesus, but whether they would *put them into practice.* Our churches are full of well-meaning people who know God's Word and can quote it from memory, but few truly live it out. Trust me that when the storms come to your house—and yes, they *will* come—knowing Scripture will not keep your house and family from falling apart. Living out the truth is what will separate your legacy from any other legacy.

How do you live out this truth? By working harder or trying harder? Believe it or not, it begins with the opposite—with resting. The "rock" in this story is Jesus' words, which is another way of saying "the gospel." Yes, this term gets lost in our modern contexts, but it is something very specific—a message about whose goodness we trust for our rescue. Is it our own? Will we trust God for heaven but live our lives as if everything else on earth is up to us? Will we worry and scramble and beg and beat ourselves into submission? Or will we let our homes be built on "nothing less than Jesus' blood and righteousness"?[1] Will we rest in the rock of Jesus' words, the message he came to deliver. We were literally dead, but he brought us life. Now our trust in his life by grace through faith gives us a strong rock—a strong foundation on which to build our lives, our marriages, and our families.

This is the *vertical* message—humbling yourself and admitting that only the grace of Jesus can rescue, redeem, and

1. Edward Mote, "My Hope Is Built on Nothing Less," 1834. Public domain.

sustain your life. You may recall the story from our first book, *Vertical Marriage*, but when Ann said to me (Dave), "I've lost my feelings for you" on our tenth anniversary, our marriage was all but over. If something didn't change right then, we were going to copy my family legacy of divorce.

Our family was headed for a "great crash."

Our marriage wasn't saved because we went to church, memorized a bunch of Bible verses, or worked our way out of it all. Our marriage was saved because we went vertical. We went to Jesus in complete brokenness and invited him to do what only he can do—namely, bring dead things to life. Jesus was gracious to grant us his *power*, surround us with his *people*, and help us put into *practice* his words; together, these elements embody a lifestyle that is dependent on him and his ways for life.

As a parent—and as a person—it's time to go vertical. Knowing what to do is not enough. It's time to surrender, and do it. It's time to stop building on things that don't last and build instead on that which can never be shaken: the grace of God revealed in the gospel of Christ. There is no better way to start creating the legacy you have dreamed about than to get on your knees right here, right now, and go vertical.

- Ask Jesus for his *power* to make you the mom or dad only he can empower you to be.
- Ask Jesus to help you find the *people* to do life with and raise your families with. Don't stop praying or seeking this until you are living intentionally in this kind of community.
- Ask Jesus to help you to put into *practice* the Word of God. We can't give away to our kids what we don't first possess. When you start with Jesus in authenticity, it will overflow from you and into your family.

Andy Stanley once said, "Your greatest contribution to the kingdom of God may not be something you do but someone you raise."[2] Just last month, our three sons and their families gathered at the funeral of Ann's mom. She was an amazing woman and a wonderful grandmother to our sons. I mean truly remarkable. As Ann and I listened to each of our three sons share memories, funny stories, and lessons learned from their beloved grandma, I thought to myself, *We are so blessed by God. Our sons are remarkable men with incredible wives and amazing children. They are all living stellar lives of impact. I can't believe that God could take two very imperfect parents like us and produce amazing—not perfect, but truly exceptional—men like this.* I prayed a simple prayer in that moment: "Thank you, Jesus, for doing what we could have never done."

There are no perfect parents and no perfect kids, but God can do *in you* and *through you* what you and I could never do apart from him. So we ask you to join us one more time on our knees to ask God to do what only he can do, first in you and then in your children. And no matter how hard it gets—and it will get extremely difficult—never give up hope. Because . . .

He has you.

And he has your kids as well.

2. Andy Stanley (@AndyStanley), Twitter post, April 17, 2013, 9:38 p.m., https://twitter.com/andystanley/status/324713440541290498.

ACKNOWLEDGMENTS

We are deeply grateful to Jesus for such special people who have loved us so well and made this book a reality.

First, we acknowledge our three sons—CJ (and Robin), Austin (and Kendall), and Cody (and Jenna). You made parenting easy and made us look like we knew what we were doing, but of course you knew we didn't have a clue.

A special thanks to Austin for not only being gracious to us as your parents but also being a killer agent. You are really good at what you do.

John Driver, who makes sense of what we write and turns it into something actually readable—you will probably find a way to make even this sentence better!

The incredible Zondervan team—David Morris, Tom Dean, Alicia Kasen, Curt Diepenhorst, Andy Rogers, Dirk Buursma, Trinity McFadden, Robin Barnett—you are the very best in the business, and we thank God for your belief in us.

FamilyLife—thank you, Dennis and Barbara Rainey, for founding such an incredible ministry that saved our marriage and gave us tools to help other families. David Robbins, Bob Lepine, and the audio team have made us better than we are and are partnering with us to create godly legacies for generations to come. Wilson Week is our favorite week of the month.

Thank you, Kensington Church, for allowing us to teach every truth in this book from the stage at Orion Campus. And though we raised our boys in a fishbowl, you gave them unrelenting grace and didn't press charges—haha!

And finally, without Debbie Popchock, our executive assistant for thirty years, we wouldn't have hit a single deadline and would still be just dreaming about writing books. You never miss a single detail, and your love for us has sustained us for years.

DAVEANDANNWILSON.COM

familylife.com @DaveAnnWilson

@daveannwilson @DaveAnnWilson

Vertical Marriage

The One Secret That Will Change Your Marriage

Dave and Ann Wilson with John Driver

Honest to the core and laugh-out-loud funny, marriage coaches Dave and Ann Wilson share the one key secret that brought them from the brink of divorce to a healthy and vibrant relationship.

He never saw it coming. It was the night of Dave and Ann's tenth wedding anniversary, and if asked how their marriage was doing, Dave would have said a 9.8 out of 10—and he even guaranteed Ann would say the same. But instead of giving him a celebratory kiss, Ann whispered, "I've lost my feelings for you."

Divorce seemed inevitable. But starting that night, God began to reveal to Dave and Ann the most overlooked secret of getting the marriage we're looking for: the horizontal marriage relationship just doesn't work until the vertical relationship with Christ is first.

As founders of a multicampus church and marriage coaches with thirty years of experience, Dave and Ann point to hard-earned but easy-to-apply biblical principles that ensure a strong marriage. Written in a highly relatable dialogue between both husband and wife, *Vertical Marriage* will guide you toward building a vibrant relationship at every level, including communication, conflict, intimacy, and romance. They share an intimate, sometimes hilarious, and deeply poignant narrative of one couple's journey to reconnecting with God and discovering the joy and power of a vertical marriage.

For anyone who is married, preparing for marriage, or desperate to save a relationship teetering on the edge of disaster, *Vertical Marriage* will give you the insight, applications, and inspiration to reconnect with God together and to transform your marriage to everything you hoped it would be.

Available in stores and online!

ZONDERVAN®
.com